Deweyan Inquiry

Deweyan Inquiry

From Education Theory to Practice

James Scott Johnston

SUNY
PRESS

Published by
State University of New York Press, Albany

© 2009 State University of New York

For information, contact State University of New York Press, Albany, NY
www.sunypress.edu

Production by Eileen Meehan
Marketing by Fran Keneston

Library of Congress Cataloging-in-Publication Data

Johnston, James Scott.
  Deweyan inquiry : from education theory to practice / James Scott Johnston.
     p. cm.
  Includes bibliographical references and index.
  ISBN 978-0-7914-9355-7 (hardcover : alk. paper)
  1. Dewey, John, 1859–1952. 2. Education—Philosophy. I. Title.

  LB875.D5J64 2009
  370.1—dc22   2008024982

10 9 8 7 6 5 4 3 2

Contents

Preface

I have written this book in hope that it is of some benefit to teacher educators, as well as practicing teachers and teacher candidates. Many, many good outlines of Dewey's educational theory exist, and I must answer to the question: Why, yet another one? This book will be of service to those who wish to see a condensed treatment of Dewey's theory and its uses in various curricular contexts. Much of the Dewey literature provides this, but not with inquiry as the central focus. Inquiry is often embedded in other concerns (reflective practice, pedagogy, the social aims of education, and the democratic classroom) and not developed with singular emphasis.

I have included some examples of how inquiry operates in relation to the various subject matters discussed. My examples are neither comprehensive nor exhaustive, and so, at the end of the book I list references that provide many better examples and strategies. My aim here is to get the reader thinking about how a teacher might use inquiry in the classroom or discuss inquiry in teacher education classes. There is voluminous literature on this subject, and I can only gesture towards it. I have included, in the footnotes, what I think are some of the best examples of this. Also in the footnotes is criticism of Dewey's approaches to inquiry in the context of the curriculum.

A final note: this book is not a substitute for Dewey's works: it is designed to stimulate teachers and teacher candidates to think of how best to use inquiry in the classroom. I recommend that, if this is used as a stand-alone text, then it be supplemented with some of Dewey's own writings—particularly as found in *Democracy and Education* or *Experience and Education*. For those wishing to concentrate on particular subject matters, I recommend reading the introduction, chapter 1, on general inquiry, and their chapter of interest.

Acknowledgments

There are several individuals I would like to thank for helping me in the preparation of this book. Thanks to Brian McAndrews, Skip Hills, Joan McDuff, and Azza Sharkawy, all at Queen's University Faculty of Education, for reading early drafts of chapters. Thanks to Azza Sharkawy (again) for directing me to Jeffrey Bloom's work on young scientists. Thanks to Lisa Chesnel, who sped this manuscript through the review process. Thanks to the reviewers at SUNY Press for their helpful suggestions. Thanks to Eileen Meehan for attempting to keep me on a tight production schedule. Special thanks to Carol for her grace, to my son, Frank, who once again put up with me while I was preparing the manuscript; to Rosa Bruno-Jofré, Dean of the Faculty of Education at Queen's University, for her never-flagging support, and to Xuemei, for love and inspiration.

Finally, this book is dedicated to Richard Rorty (1931–2007). I met Dick several times at various conferences, beginning in the late 1990's, and we spoke on the phone and conversed through email on several occasions. Dick is quite rightly responsible for the resurgence of interest in Dewey scholarship, largely through the publication of *Philosophy and the Mirror of Nature*, *Consequences of Pragmatism*, and his collected papers. I had the good fortune to tell him so on one occasion. His views on Dewey are to say the least, contentious. However, all agree that through his influence, Dewey is once again a force to be reckoned with in American philosophy, education, and social science.

The author wishes to acknowledge the Board of Trustees, Southern Illinois University and Southern Illinois University Press, for the selections from *The Collected Works of John Dewey*.

Introduction

The aim of this book is to help provide teacher educators, practicing teachers, and teacher candidates with an understanding of inquiry in the context of schooling. The understanding I hope to facilitate is the aims, points, purposes, and practices of conscious, deliberate inquiry on the part of both teacher and student into subject matters. The inquiry I discuss is that conceived by John Dewey. The schooling I refer to is inclusive of primary, middle, and secondary grades. The contexts I draw on are science (inclusive of mathematics); social science (inclusive of history and geography); art (inclusive of poetry and literature); and physical education (inclusive of team and individual sports, athletics, dance, and theatre). A discussion of the general features of inquiry common to all contexts is also provided.

THE CASE FOR INQUIRY

It has become a cliché to say that we want teachers to be 'critical thinkers' and 'reflective practitioners.' These are clichés not only in the sense that they are ideals (even platitudes) bandied about with little thought to what they mean in practice, but also they are frequently unsupported in fact. The sad truth of the matter is that few teachers are actually encouraged to become responsible, inquiring professionals and those that do, do so largely on their own, without supervisory encouragement. This is not because they are not told to be reflective or critical; nor is it because they are not encouraged to read, to think about their practice, or to question. All of these characteristics, and more, are stressed and expected, especially of teacher candidates. However, the reality of the schools and the reality of teachers' colleges and colleges of education are, as most everyone well knows, very different.

What happens when one begins to work in a school? Sadly, much of the idealism, together with the critical eye that students are encouraged to use and develop, is put aside, even crushed. The working environment and its needs and expectations take over. What seems to be an overbearing and fixed bureaucratic set of curricular and performance expectations washes away whatever opportunities new teachers have to make meaningful, existential changes in their teaching practices, let alone in the curriculum. To put it bluntly, schools, and the vast, bureaucratic system behind them, block the road to inquiry. To ask teachers, both novice and veteran, what needs to be done to develop children who have a love for learning, an insatiable appetite for inquiry, and a disposition to care about and try to solve social problems, is to receive no shortage of solid answers. These answers, sadly, cannot be enacted. My point here is not to engage in a screed against systems of education. It is rather to suggest that the task of becoming a critical practitioner is difficult. However, I do not believe that it is insurmountable. Despite the difficulties, good teachers reach students and influence their own practices through reflection and through conscious and deliberate uses of inquiry. What is needed for this to transpire beyond institutional support is a framework or model of how inquiry can be of use in the classroom.

Why would teachers want to get serious about inquiry? Because the more developed and refined the inquiry a child brings to bear on an educational problem, the more likely she is to solve that problem. Beyond the psychological benefits of gratification, intrinsic motivation, and the esteem that this provides, a refined and developed inquiry lends itself to new problems and new contexts, and, if inquiry is developed and practiced, it eventually leads to the development of solid academic dispositions. I want to be clear that inquiry is neither a panacea, nor a cure for social ills; nor can inquiry, in isolation, result in school success: no single educational endeavour could claim this. The need to justify changes in current practice is paramount: too much tinkering towards utopia (to use David Tyack and Larry Cuban's clever turn of phrase), goes on in the name of school practice and it is doubtful that much of it, in isolation, actually makes a practical difference to student success. A focused, deliberate framework and a program that is in keeping with the point and purposes of inquiry can augment a child's successful understanding of the world. All things being equal, inquiry has the capacity to do good for children providing its implementation is thoroughgoing.

No doubt, there are many educational models of inquiry from which to choose. Many of these are valuable adjuncts to teaching practice. These better models stress pedagogically appropriate instruction and do so in the context of our accumulated knowledge of biology, psychology, sociology, and culture. Additionally, these models foreground their philosophy of education; there is a rich set of moral, ethical, and existential beliefs about human beings, social groups, and humanity. An accommodating model of inquiry requires these features; to do without these is to surrender the reasons we educate in the first place. As I show, Dewey's theory of inquiry has all of this.

THE CASE FOR DEWEYAN INQUIRY

What makes Dewey's theory of inquiry ideal for schools is, first, its sensitivity. Dewey's theory of inquiry is context-bound: it is not a method brought down from on high to bear on all educational practices or problems. Rather, it is a set of methods, built up in and through contexts which they serve, for the purposes of understanding, ordering, and controlling, our experiences of, and our relations with, the world. Second, Dewey's theory of inquiry is self-correcting: it is designed to adjust itself in light of anticipated and unanticipated changes in educational practice. This makes Dewey's theory of inquiry more user-friendly than might otherwise be imagined; it can be developed in and through a variety of contexts. Third, it is driven by problems. These problems are the problems of the child, not the problems of the teacher, or the textbook, or the state, meaning it is the child's interest and effort guiding inquiry; inquiry is finished when there is no longer the unsettled situation that gave rise to inquiry in the first place.

These three attributes of inquiry I shall discuss at more length in the chapters that follow. In this book, I want to discuss why I believe inquiry to be an important (though neglected) topic for educational practice. Certainly educational psychologists and curriculum specialists have dealt with, and recommended, various models of inquiry over the decades, and many of these have found their way into schools of education, staff development programs, programmed instructional material, not to mention the trade journals. This is correct, as far as it goes. Seldom, though, is a thoroughgoing attempt made to develop the insights into inquiry that would lead to a conscious program that can be adopted by and for, schools. No doubt part of this is due to the various contexts in which the inquiry is used: one size inquiry does not fit all, and this is as it should be. However, what is also missing is the wherewithal to carry out a program of inquiry that could be sensitive to these contexts. Such an inquiry has been developed, can be understood, and can be carried out.

Deweyan models of inquiry, like Deweyan models of the curriculum, of discipline, and of teaching and learning, are not well established in schools, despite rhetoric to the contrary in colleges of education. In fact, Deweyan models of inquiry, as with these other models, have never fully caught on in public schools. The dominant model(s) of inquiry have been behaviourist: this state of affairs has its legacy in the efficiency movement of the early twentieth century, and despite variances, has remained with us since.[1] The preoccupation of testing students is a contemporary example of this. Models that come close to Dewey's are available and are in practice. Problem-based and discovery learning, as well as the trend towards a democratic classroom, are good examples of a broadly Deweyan approach to inquiry. However, even these programs are scattered: the impetus to take these on and run with them is simply not there. Indeed, the efficiency model notwithstanding, it is doubtful if any model is consistently adhered to, given the contradictory agendas and competing rhetoric impressing themselves on teachers and administrators. The institutional obstacles preventing even a piecemeal commitment to a Deweyan inquiry do militate against its usefulness: of this, there can be no question. Nevertheless, at the pain of giving up hope for a more effective, productive, and humane educational experience for students, we continue to develop strategies to improve.

CHAPTER SUMMARIES

Inquiry varies with the contexts in which it is used. It is, therefore, loosely circular; the contexts partly determine what will count as techniques and methods, and techniques and methods will alter the context. It is important to identity just what these techniques and methods are, and what inquiry, considered generally, does with these. It is also important to identify what contexts count as those that inquiry participates in. Chapter 1 sets out to define inquiry, discuss its methods and techniques, and the contexts in which it is used.

Once the contexts are identified, it becomes necessary to examine how inquiry functions within that specific context. Chapter 2 examines inquiry in the context of science and science education—education specifically associated with active investigation and experimentation of the natural and physical world. Inquiry differs in this context from all others in the preciseness of its techniques, the deliberate nature of its problem-solving, and the care with which propositions, definitions, and arguments are constructed. This is not to say that inquiry, in the context of science, is the best or highest form of inquiry: far from it. Rather, it is to say that scientific inquiry is the most self-conscious of these modes.

In chapter 3, I examine inquiry in society and social science education. Here I am thinking primarily of geography and history, but not to the exclusion of other subject matters or courses that might intersect with social-scientific topics. As inquiry in social science education looks different than inquiry in science, it is important to note what distinguishes these two from one another. It was Dewey's greatest hope that the social sciences would embrace the experimental method with the same rigour and consistency as the natural and physical sciences. What this looks like and how this might work is the focus of this chapter.

In chapter 4, I examine inquiry in a context very different from the scientific: the context of art. Dewey has a great deal to say about art and aesthetic experience in particular. Inquiry plays a key role in how an artist practices, as well as how an (aesthetic) experience may be enriched. Both of these are of interest to us. Beyond this, inquiry in the context of art tells us something about the role of emotion and imagination in inquiry writ large, a connection that is often lacking in outcomes-based educational research.

Finally, in chapter 5, I examine the relationship of inquiry to physical education and psychomotor practices. This includes not only athletics and sports but dance, theatre, and performance art. I subsume these practices under the label, "bodily-kinesthetics." By this term, I connote the interconnection of inquiry and bodily movement (including psychomotor development) through habit and practice. What inquiry looks like in this context, and how it can be marshalled to support further and better physical and psychomotor development, is the focus here.

In the conclusion, I return to my initial thesis: that inquiry requires much more deliberate attention than it is currently receiving. I highlight and summarize the arguments of the preceding chapters to demonstrate why this is so. I also set out some suggestions as to how and where inquiry might be better utilized in classrooms, and how it might be incorporated in the various contexts in which it is used.

CHAPTER ONE

An Account of General Inquiry

Dewey's last and most famous statement on inquiry, which, for the purposes of this book, is synonymous with method comes in his late tour de force, *Logic: the Theory of Inquiry*.[2] There, he claims:

> Inquiry is the controlled or directed transformation of an indeterminate situation into one that is so determinate in its constituent distinctions and relations as to convert the elements of the original situation into a unified whole. (LW 12 1938, p. 108)

Prior to this highly generalized conception of inquiry (which I shall discuss more fully momentarily) is the claim that,

> inquiry, in spite of the diverse subjects to which it applies, and the consequent diversity of its special techniques, has a common structure or pattern: that this common structure is applied both in common sense and science, although because of the nature of the problems with which they are concerned, the emphasis upon the factors involved varies widely in the two modes. (LW 12 1938, p. 105)

Further, Dewey tells us that,

> The search for the pattern of inquiry is, accordingly, not one instituted in the dark or at large. It is checked and controlled by the knowledge of the kinds of inquiry that have and that have not worked; methods which . . . can be so compared as to yield reasoned or rational conclusions. (LW 12 1938, p. 108)

Elsewhere and in a different context, Dewey writes:

> When it is understood that philosophic thinking is caught up
> in the actual course of events, having the office of guiding them
> towards a prosperous issue, problems will abundantly present
> themselves. Philosophy will not solve these problems; philosophy
> is vision, imagination, reflection—and these functions, apart from
> action, modify nothing and hence resolve nothing . . . Philosophy
> recovers itself when it ceases to be a device for dealing with
> the problems of philosophers and becomes a *method*, cultivated
> by philosophers, for dealing with the *problems of men*. (MW 10
> 1916–1917, p. 46. Italics mine)

What I urge is that we take these four statements of Dewey's, run them
together, and take the final product to be inquiry. When we do this; when
we run these four statements together, we get something like this:

1. Inquiry transforms problematic situations into understandable
   and manageable ones. When we inquire, we develop distinctions
   and relations out of the situation that allow us to see through
   problems.

2. Inquiry is inclusive of common sense and science, and has varying techniques, though there is a common structure (or pattern)
   to inquiry.

3. Past inquiries are (in part) the context for further inquiries.
   We use what we have already learned in present and future problem solving.

4. Inquiry helps to solve "the problems of men": inquiry helps solve
   social problems.

As I discuss inquiry, these are the senses I shall rely on. All inquiry is trans-
formative; inquiry involves discriminating, analyzing, relating; inquiry takes
place (in part) in the context of past inquiries, and inquiry is guided by the
problems it aims to solve. We can take these broad points as what is common
to inquiry regardless of the contexts in which it is used and developed. So
for example, whether inquiry is used in a laboratory experiment undertaken
in a grade 10 science classroom, or helping children to grasp a reading lesson
in grade 3, these features or characteristics of inquiry will be present.

What I want to show in the rest of this chapter is how general method
or inquiry, works. I will do this by examining three angles to inquiry: what
inquiry consists in, or has as its features; where inquiry operates, or its

contexts; and the mechanics of inquiry; what makes it tick. Discussing the first of these angles involves noting which techniques, practices, attitudes, and tempers are required for inquiry; discussing the second of these involves noting the sorts of problems inquiry is called on to help solve; and discussing the third of these involves examining the logic of inquiry proper; how we form and handle conceptions, abstractions, propositions, and inferences.

OF WHAT DOES INQUIRY CONSIST

Perhaps the best statement on general inquiry in the context of education comes from Dewey's most famous work, *Democracy and Education*. Here, Dewey says,

> Such matters as knowledge of the past, of current technique, of materials, of the ways in which one's own best results are assured, supply the material for what may be called *general* method. There exists a cumulative body of fairly stable methods for reaching results, a body authorized by past experience and by intellectual analysis, which an individual ignores at his peril. (MW 9 1916, p. 177)

I want to discuss just what each of these matters amounts to. I begin with knowledge of the past. We can take this in several senses. The first sense might be knowledge of our individual immediate past. How have we handled problems in our own situations and circumstances? We often have a clue to our future problem-solving performances in our past attempts. The habits, if you will, of problem-solving tend to set in early and become reinforced, and as every educator knows, can be terribly difficult to break. One of the ways education can help head off the development of bad problem-solving habits is (characteristically enough) to help children develop good ones to begin with. Developed early on, these good problem-solving habits can then be used to develop further good habits.

The second sense of knowledge of the past is that knowledge is accumulated: that is to say, it is the combined knowledge of the group, classroom, school, community, nation, and culture. Accumulated knowledge is so not only by virtue of repositories of information but also so by virtue of oral customs and traditions, passed down from generation to generation in one's social group(s). Often, as the teachers of children, we are the ones that present this accumulated knowledge of the past. What we have learned is passed along to the next generation. This is not to say that education has its functions and purposes exhausted in transmitting traditions or knowledge; rather, one of the functions of education is to provide this.

The third sense of knowledge of the past is experimental and reconstructive. We chide those that teach by rote, and emphasize drills, memorization, and recitation over and against group work. We applaud discovery learning, and learning by doing. Why? One reason is that we believe that rote does not accomplish what it sets out to do: fashion students into critical thinkers. The question is of course, how do we fashion students to be critical and reflective thinkers? An often-heard answer is that we do so by having children actively engage in the subject matter at hand. A ready-to-hand example is the calculation of force in a physics experiment: the student actually works with materials, observes changes in distance, et cetera, and calculates the force involved. In other words, she experiments. Nevertheless, not only does she experiment, she reproduces and reconstructs. We can reproduce experiments that led to significant gains in scientific understanding. We can drop balls with Galileo, or learn how to use a manometer with Torricelli; we can see how difficult it would be for the early Americans to survive in the winter with little food and shelter by role-playing aspects of this. Reconstructive knowledge of the past involves investigating the problem-solving strategies of past peoples, to see where they went wrong, where they got it right, and how we can improve on their strategies. Reconstructive knowledge of the past takes the past and uses it in the context of the present.

Current technique is the next feature of general inquiry. When we think of techniques, we are to think of the ways and means we problem-solve. These ways, of course, differ depending upon the problem. One would not think of trying to solve a problem involving the angle of incidence of light hitting water by reading Shakespeare for insight; for the same reason, understanding the grammar of sentences is probably of little help to a student attempting to learn trigonometry. Mathematical methods are often called for in experimental science; seldom are they called for in literature classes. Likewise, techniques of character and plot analysis would be of little benefit in the physics classroom. The point is that there is an assemblage of built-up techniques, common to the various contexts that are used to problem solve in those contexts. What is general about inquiry across these contexts is that there are techniques that we draw on when we problem-solve and, for the most part, these are successful in aiding us in our goal. I discuss the situation in which they prove unacceptable further on in this chapter.

Some of the more common techniques are theories (how and why does the world operate the way it does?; how and why do we humans operate the way we do?; how can we categorize our findings about a subject-matter?). Others include mathematical methods designed to handle large amounts of data, or develop sophisticated means of relating disparate data. Still others involve observational and interpretative strategies (often of use in the social sciences) such as empathy or 'putting oneself in another's shoes.' There is also textual analysis and interpretation (often of use in the humanities); logic; communication patterns and strategies, including the dissemination of scholarly literature; guidance and facilitation; and the list goes on. It is important to see these techniques as tools, as means to further the problem-solving process. They are not ends in themselves. Mathematics for example, developed out of and is used for problem-solving existential and social crises, and continues to be used this way, notwithstanding those scholar-mathematicians that delight in abstraction. The question of the role of abstraction in general inquiry is an important one, and I consider this further on in the chapter.

What counts as materials? The subject matter that inquiry has as its focus comes to mind first. We may say for example, that motion or Hamlet's indecision is the subject matter at hand. We can be more general or more specific, as the problem we are trying to solve, and the context calls for. Obviously, the materials involved in constructing a light experiment (track, ball, ruler, watch, etc.), and understanding Shakespeare (the play *Hamlet*, secondary sources, a performance, etc.), are different. But note that in both cases, materials are needed at various stages. Of course, we need to be able to experiment with motion, and this requires certain implements, but we also need to be able to measure the results, and these require other implements. Likewise, we need to be able to read *Hamlet*, and this requires access to the play. But we also need to be able to discuss *Hamlet*, and this requires a classroom, a teacher, other students, and perhaps secondary sources. In both cases, implements or as I shall call them, *tools*, are involved. These tools stretch from the material to the immaterial. If we consider our observations, measurements, and analyses, indeed, our thoughts, concepts, and behaviors as tools, we begin to see the manifold nature of materials.

Our own best results are assured by the successes of our inquiries: this seems circular. Is it not the case that best results are the successes of our inquiries? This is correct, until we qualify this through a definition of success. What counts as a successful solution to problems is the satisfaction (Dewey calls it a unified whole) that results. This is not to be taken as merely an emotional response, though it is inclusive of emotion. It is cognitive, behavioural, and affective. Further, it leads to future successes: we now have a method we can apply in different contexts to see if it solves these problems. If our method is sound, and we are able to adjust it accordingly, we may just develop from this a habit of inquiring that is made a routine feature of our general dispositions. This is what Dewey hopes formal education will do for children: provide them with opportunities such that they can develop the habits of inquiry so that they might then have strong and robust problem-solving dispositions.

There are two more characteristics of inquiry that are important to mention, though not dealt with in the above quotation of Dewey's. The first of these is the attitude or temper of inquiry; the second is self-correction. Dewey talks about attitudes in another famous work, *How We Think*. Here, Dewey says:

> Because of the importance of attitudes, ability to train thought is not achieved merely by knowledge of the best forms of thought. Possession of this information is no guarantee for ability to think well. Moreover, there are no set exercises in correct thinking whose repeated performance will cause one to be a good thinker. The information and the exercises are both of value. But no individual realizes their value except as he is personally animated by certain dominant attitudes in his own character . . . It is a matter of common notice that men who are expert thinkers in their own special fields adopt views on other matters without doing the inquiring that they know to be necessary for substantiating simpler facts that fall within their own specialties. (LW 8 1933, p. 135)

We may think of the high school physics teacher who has an (uninformed) opinion of immigration matters, let us say. She believes that immigration ought to be curtailed and certain people kept out of the country, a position based, not on her expertise but on personal opinion or on the opinion of others. The problem occurs when a noted authority takes a public position on an issue, without the requisite background in, and attitudes necessary for, fair and impartial inquiry. Likewise, a teacher who does not have the attitudes necessary for textual interpretation may use his or her authority to pronounce on some matter in literature. For example, let us say: "I don't see what good Shakespeare does anybody; why can't we just have children learn science?" Common to both of these scenarios is a lack of the proper attitude for inquiry in and for that context. As inquiry takes place in different contexts and calls upon differing techniques, materials, and tools (including thinking tools), it equally calls on attitudes congenial to different contexts. Some of these attitudes, as with techniques, are difficult to transpose from one context to another and recognizing this can forestall premature judgments of value.

The other notable conclusion Dewey draws in the above passage regards the role of character. Character is a necessary ingredient in inquiry. There is no guarantee that an English teacher will, because she possesses the skills, attitudes, and techniques for interpreting twentieth-century American literature, have the attitude for conducting chemistry experiments. There is certainly valuable information and techniques to be gained through practice, as Dewey says. Moreover, some of these may even be transposable to other contexts. This transposition, however, is limited; but there is no substitute for information and exercise internal to one's context of inquiry.

The other important characteristic is self-correction. This means that inquiry has the capacity to adjust itself when its findings are not in accord with its hoped for or anticipated results, and a capacity to adjust itself to the contexts in which it is in and is used. As problems are the proper matter of inquiry, and these problems are very often social problems, it is the consequences of enacting the results of the inquiry that determine what way to go. Dewey provides support for this. For example, Dewey claims:

> Just as the validity of a proposition in discourse, or of conceptual material generally, cannot be determined short of the consequences to which its functional use gives rise, so the sufficient warrant of a judgment as a claimant to knowledge . . . cannot be determined apart from connection with a widening circle of consequences . . . Until agreement upon consequences is reached by those who reinstate the conditions set forth, the conclusions that are announced by an individual inquirer have the status of hypothesis, especially if the findings fail to agree with the general trend of already accepted results. (LW 13 1938, p. 484)

We cannot foreswear the consequences of the conclusions of judgments we make. If I conclude a student is malingering because she shows up to class fifteen minutes late, then I am setting in motion consequences for her, myself, and the class. Some of these consequences will prove to be relatively benign. It probably will not cause a great disruption if I recommence my lesson after a moment. However, the judgment I make may lead me to make other judgments, or commit to other actions that are not so benign. For example, I may alter my impression of the student and carry this alternation with me in subsequent evaluations. In a laboratory context, my conclusions may not be in accord with the conclusions of others, and as a result they may be invalid. Note that the justifiers for consequences anticipated are not the individual experimenters: it is the community of experimenters. The justification for what counts as consequences (as well as when the consequences are broached) is social. I shall discuss this in detail shortly.

THE CONTEXTS OF INQUIRY

Thus far, we have discussed that inquiry must be sensitive to the contexts in which it is found and used. We have maintained that inquiry must self-correct: Inquiry must consider what the consequences of a settled result will be, and adjust itself accordingly. This means that, with the exception of some general features, inquiry will look quite different in different contexts. Indeed, though contexts are many, they are all contexts in which a potential problem arises. The seemingly limitless expanse of contexts makes inquiry across these a difficult undertaking, as inquiry is required to be sensitive to consequences in the particular context in which it is found and used, and to self-adjust accordingly. Many of the tools used in one context will not work in another, and to avoid difficulties requires deliberate and careful selection of techniques.

Fortunately, we are not frequently called upon to inquire deliberately and deeply into a manifold of contexts. There are several contexts, though, that Dewey thinks are important to inquire into, and that all citizens should have facility in. For the purposes of educating children, these are:

1. experimentation under and in laboratory conditions and contexts (science)

2. aesthetic contexts (art, music, and literature—making and doing)

3. interpersonal contexts (classmates, authority figures, friends, and relatives)

4. Public contexts (other citizens in a community, the larger community, and beyond).

5. Bodily-kinesthetic contexts involving awareness and psychomotor control

Schools have the responsibility and opportunity to facilitate the development of inquiry in each and all of these contexts. This is so because each and all of these contexts are necessary for the physical, emotional, intellectual, and social growth of the child. Sadly, administrative needs and misguided legislation often demand that the first context take precedent over the others; when this is done, it is at the cost of others. What often results is a narrow and truncated view of what counts as a legitimate problem, legitimate context, and legitimate tools and attitudes. One cannot simply transpose the techniques and methods of laboratory science onto, for example, problems of a public nature, and expect the appropriate consequences to ensue. While experimenting on the capacity of acids to damage foliage in a classroom yields potentially valuable information, it does not produce valid consequences for nonlaboratory settings. One must develop new problem-finding and solving techniques and methods, and continue to work in the context of problems of a public nature for this to occur.

I discuss each of these contexts briefly, and spend much more time with all of these in subsequent chapters. Here, I provide a rough summary of what the tools and techniques in each of these might look like, and what sorts of consequences inquiry aims for in using these. To begin with, laboratory science of the sort practiced in physics, chemistry, and biology classes, aims at precision and the accuracy of measured findings. Often these findings are data—measurable changes in phenomena studied. The tools for being able to measure changes in phenomena are varied, but at some level, mathematics is necessary to gather and organize the data into a quantified statement, easily reproducible and understood by others. As well, tools to manipulate the environment to effect desired changes in phenomena are required. These can be anything from balls and inclines to a supercollider. Most importantly, but often neglected, are the frameworks, theories, and conceptions generated in and through laboratory science. Helping a biology student to understand homeostais is not to help a student to an easily identifiable or measurable bit of data; it is to teach a student to understand the functions of a living organism in such a way that she can make sense of disparate phenomena and changes in physiology. Homeostasis functions as a model of disparate events.

Aesthetic concerns are another neglected context of inquiry. This is sad, particularly because helping a child to reach aesthetic fulfillment and satisfaction is a sure way to encourage further inquiry and the development of good dispositions. What we mean by aesthetic is, for my purposes, construed as experiential. To say aesthetic, then, is to say that one has a certain sort or quality of experience, a highly satisfactory experience. The sort of aha moment, when a student gets it, would qualify as aesthetic. Teachers also have these moments: A particularly successful class is one wherein the students grasp a difficult lesson or concept. Moments such as these are often what carry us forward in our teaching practices. Dewey often connects aesthetic inquiry to making and doing: art, music, building, designing, and developing. But it need not be confined to these alone. Reflection can be equally aesthetic. What makes something aesthetic as opposed to humdrum is the quality of the experience had.

Interpersonal concerns are also neglected, though much educational literature has seen the need for attention to these.[3] It does no good to promote experimental inquiry and at the same time neglect to help students develop the interpersonal skills needed to solve complex problems—problems that simply cannot be solved by isolated individuals. The skills needed to solve complex problems in interpersonal settings cannot be transposed with facility. The image of a solitary scientist alone, working furiously through the night in his laboratory is quaint, but misleading. Scientists test their work not only in the laboratory, but in trade journals, and this requires a community of scholars. Furthermore, laboratory science cannot take place without a cadre of administrators, students, assistants, and apprentices. More generally, it stands to reason that, if we want to solve social problems, then we cannot do so in isolation from one another. Social problems demand social solutions, and these solutions are premised on the capacity for groups that have the problem to come together to solve the problem. Inquiry in these contexts must focus on the skills of communication, dialogue, and the development of a shared and sympathetic set of sentiments toward others. Large projects, exacting laboratory experiments, and sport strategies are often done in groups, not simply for the sake of efficiency, but for the creative, imaginative, and critical resources others provide.

Issues of public concern ought to be at the forefront of inquiry. I say this because we often claim that we want the public to be informed and educated about problems (for this is a large part of what democracy consists in), but equally because inquiry has more success if it is done in a public, open, manner, rather than in isolation or behind the scenes. I also add that what goes for interpersonal problems goes for public ones as well: Public problems demand public solutions. When we teach students about citizenship, human rights, civics, law and government, and the historical treatment of immigrants and the poor, for example, we do so because we want students to see that the problems generated in each of these areas are problems common to us all. If we want citizens who inquire publicly (and Dewey does), then we must help them develop the attitudes and techniques of public inquiry. Some of these are coeval with inquiry in interpersonal contexts—communication, dialogue, and a shared and sympathetic set of attitudes toward those who cannot effectively solve their problems. But an understanding of the procedural and administrative facets of democracies (in the context of Europe, North America, and other Western, liberal nations), their histories and past problems, and the means of alleviating these problems, will also be required.

One of the great tragedies of public education (at least in North America) is the ongoing relegation of physical education to the periphery. This is tragic, particularly considering the health issues we currently face. Developing bodily-kinesthetic habits is a task every bit as demanding and time-consuming as developing the habits of aesthetic or scientific inquiry, and every bit as important. Inquiry is as pervasive in the former context as it is in the latter two. If anything, inquiry is more difficult, because there is seldom time to linger over possible consequences. Movement demands immediate attention and action, and the wrong movement portends injury. The benefits of bodily-kinesthetic inquiry are manifold: healthy bodies; satisfying experiences; collegial relations (team sports, clubs, outings); and increased alertness for more traditionally intellectual modes of life.

HOW THE LOGIC OF INQUIRY OPERATES

Thus far, we have discussed the nature of inquiry, the techniques and tools of inquiry, and the contexts of inquiry. Here, I want to focus on the guts of inquiry—the logic that inquiry uses from the beginning to the end of problem-solving. This logic will differ depending upon the contexts, but what I present here can generally be found in inquiry operating in any context. By logic, I do not mean the formal logic often taught in college courses for math credit. Dewey's understanding of logic is not solely mathematical. In fact, Dewey thinks that the mathematicization of logic has prevented otherwise intelligent practitioners from seeing the contexts in which logic takes place, and even more importantly, the point of logic. Logic is a means to solve problems; not an intellectual end in itself. Dewey thinks that logicians often forget that logic's primary function is to settle situations. I draw from Dewey's, *Logic: the Theory of Inquiry*.

We begin the path of inquiry when we are confronted with an indeterminate situation (LW 13 1938, p. 109). We do not grasp a particular bit of a situation and label that indeterminate—Dewey is quite clear about this. Rather, the situation in its entirety is what is indeterminate: Indeterminacy is a synonym for doubt; the sort of doubt that philosopher Charles S. Peirce once called an irritation. An irritation prompts us to scratch. Likewise, indeterminacy compels us to look for a settlement. An indeterminate situation is not yet inquiry though, only when

> existential consequences are anticipated; when environing con-
> ditions are examined with reference to their potentialities; and
> when responsive activities are selected and ordered with reference
> to actualization of some of the potentialities, rather than others,
> in a "final existential situation," is inquiry properly speaking,
> begun. (LW 13 1938, p. 111)

When we anticipate consequences, we try to think ahead to what they will accomplish. We think of manipulating our environments to effect a potential improvement. We contemplate what the actualization of this manipulation will accomplish. When we have a deliberate focus, we are in a position to say that there is a problem. Another way to put this is to say that problem finding is prior to problem solving. The indeterminate situation is just that; a situation. It is not yet a problem until a judgment that a situation is problematic, occurs (LW 13 1938, p. 111–12). The task now is to judge the right problem—that is to say, to determine that the problem is, in fact, in concert with the indeterminate situation. Much of our time and energy is wasted in labelling an existential situation improperly: we judge the wrong problem to be the case. The classic educational example concerns a child's performance on a test: did the child do poorly because she is unprepared, or because she did not sleep sufficiently well last night? Only investigation will result in a determination. We would be judging the wrong problem if we did not collect enough information to label the existential situation properly. Because the conception of the problem determines what consequences we will entertain, we have the potential to do damage and waste time and resources if the initial judgment is faulty. Likewise, to set up a problem where no problem exists is an exercise in futility.

The important concern here is that the problem is to be a genuine one—that it reflects the indeterminate situation out of which it develops. Genuine problems tie directly to the indeterminate situation and have consequences that follow (though not always directly) from the judgment. My favourite educational example of the development of a nongenuine problem is the recent return of the high-stakes testing movement in the United States. In this case, it developed in response to perceived differences in academic performance across the globe. Rather than questioning whether there was a problem with differences in test scores that made a difference to students or teachers, legislators and government officials presented the public with both a problem and its solution—curiously enough, more test-ing of children, the very practice that had sparked the problem in the first place! Instead of a genuine problem, the public of the United States was provided with an illusory one. Sadly, Canada (at least Ontario) seems to be marching headlong into the same battlefield.

Once a problem has been identified, a solution or set of solutions is anticipated. This requires finding what Dewey calls definite constituents, constituents of a situation that are settled (LW 13 1938, p. 112). Another way to put this is that we must find settled, existential (real) traits. We generally do this through observation and/or measurement. What counts as a solution to the problem, then, will be some improvement in the situation, notable through observed changes in traits. In other words (and this is the important conclusion to draw), solutions to problems are existential. In the context of education, that usually means an improvement in behaviour, or performance on evaluations, or a change in the self-report of a student (for the better). Along the way, more subtle improvements may occur, and it is important that these be picked up on.

There is of course, a role for ideas: ideas are the anticipated conse-quences that will then be carried out in practice (LW 13 1938, p. 113). An idea is a possibility. As we move further along the path of inquiry, some ideas are jettisoned, others are kept and strengthened. Ideas differ according to their consequences. What counts as a good idea is the instrumental force of the consequences it bears out. At the level of ideas, however, what counts as consequences is not existential: it is anticipated to have the preferred existential import, but this evaluative undertaking has not yet happened. What counts as a consequence for ideas is how well they hook onto each other, how well they relate to each other such that a coherent model or framework is constructed (LW 13 1938, p. 115). Depending on the context in which the ideas are formed and tested, these may be of a more or less abstract nature. Consider the abstraction of Einstein's theory of general relativity versus Newton's: we can see Newton's theory of motion at work in a way we cannot with Einstein. The subject matter at hand plays a large role in determining this: sometimes high degrees of abstraction are required to solve the problem at hand.

Ideas that pan out are those that (circularly) are meaningfully related to one another. The next step is to see whether or not these ideas can be operationalized. To operationalize an idea is to test it out in an existential situation—the situation that we determine is a problem. This is what we commonly refer to as experimentation.

> Ideas are operational in that they instigate and direct further operations of observation; they are proposals and plans for acting upon existing conditions to bring new facts to light and to organize all the selected facts into a coherent whole. (LW 13 1938, p. 116)

Some ideas are operationalized when they lead to other, further operations that terminate in an existential change. A student confronting a difficult passage in Shakespeare's *Julius Caesar* may require additional ideas beyond those already developed in the context of the classroom if he is to write a successful paper. He may wish to investigate, for example, the history of the Roman Republic to get some indication of what was at stake in Caesar declaring himself, emperor. He will formulate an idea of Roman government that leads him to another idea—perhaps a set of purported reasons for Caesar's murder. He can develop these in the context of his paper.

Some ideas lead directly to an existential change. Consider the following examples. In a grade 5 classroom, a teacher wishes to have students understand homonyms. An explanation is given: homonyms are words that sound the same, but are spelled differently. The child takes this rule and works through existential situations, actually identifying homonyms correctly. This is a fairly simple and direct example. Consider a more complicated one. A grade 12-advanced chemistry teacher attempts to explain the concept of angular momentum. Because this deals with wave mechanics—a postulated, indirectly measurable, but nevertheless nonobservational attempt at understanding how smaller particles move in orbit around larger ones—the idea of angular momentum can only be connected to the idea of wave mechanics, which in turn is connected to the idea of quantum mechanics, which is in turn connected to the idea of subatomic particles; atomic particles and so on. Note that measurement here is at best indirect: there is no directly observable particle for the student to note. She must see that the idea makes sense in the context of other, meaningful ideas, and that this idea has its consequence in capturing a better sense of what is going on than another idea (say, the movement of subparticulate matter as God's plan) might.

Let's spend a bit of time looking closely at what counts as an idea. Dewey tells us that ideas are meaningful relations. These are thought-relations, relations that are born out of the circumstances of reflecting on anticipated consequences and the means to obtain them. Dewey distinguishes between two relations: conceptions and propositions. I discuss propositions first. When we make a statement or a sentence, we are making a proposition. It is raining, or the snow is white, or Johnny cannot read, are all propositions. What makes these propositions is that they are statements of what we believe to be the case. These are statements to be tested existentially; that is, concretely. We can ask: Is it the case that Johnny cannot read? How would we know? We must test this proposition. When we make propositions in inquiry, we make claims about what is in fact the case. We can call these existential propositions or, as Dewey sometimes does, generic propositions.

Existential or generic propositions are often propositions of classes or kinds. We use these to sort, order, and classify existential traits, data, phenomena et cetera. Take the example of a high school biology class in which students learn to classify various members of the animal kingdom under a rule. What constitutes a human being? What distinguishes a human being from some other animal? What, in short, is a defining characteristic of a human being? Propositions of these sorts are often of the all-some variety. For example: All human beings have opposable thumbs. John has opposable thumbs. John is a human being.

We can construct this logical statement precisely because we can classify those having opposable thumbs as human beings. The inability to do this would jeopardize the conclusion that John is, indeed, a member of this class.

Let's consider an example from English literature: Hamlet is an adult male. Hamlet loves and wants to marry his mother. Adult males want to marry their mothers. This second proposition is demonstrably false. It hinges on the conclusion that, because Hamlet wants to marry his mother and Hamlet is an adult male, all adult males wish to marry their mothers. As an existential proposition (and contra Ernest Jones), this generic proposition fails.

Existential propositions do not occur in a vacuum. Where does the license to form a generic proposition come from in the first place? The answer is a conception. Think of a conception as a rule that states, if such and such occurs, then this and that will follow, or whenever Johnny does behaviour X, he gets in trouble. When we make a conception, we are making what Dewey calls a universal—a rule that claims that something just *is* the case, given certain specifying conditions. It is under these rules that generic propositions operate. We can say, for example, that Johnny cannot read, because we have the prior conception that, if Johnny hasn't eaten his breakfast, he will not concentrate on his reading. Given that Johnny has not had breakfast this morning, the existential proposition, Johnny cannot read, follows. The question that remains is, can Johnny read otherwise than this?

Of course, conceptions are often much more complex than this. Philosophical conceptions, in particular, are notorious for being abstract and difficult to operationalize. Consider the concepts of humanity or dignity; these are frequently mentioned ideas in social science classes on civics or law and government. What gives these concepts the authority to operate? The reason they function is that many different generic or existential propositions can comfortably fit under them, or work with them. The conception, humanity, has done a lot for concrete changes in peoples' lives. This is the cash value, so to speak, of this conception. It has led to existential propositions that provide us with ways to develop better living conditions for human beings. What gives abstract conceptions their operational strength is their ability to generate workable existential propositions that have a tangible effect on human conduct.

Consider the following: Natural Selection better helps us account for the variety of species than does the notion of fixed kinds.

Current, yet misleading controversies regarding science and religion to the contrary, Natural Selection is a working solution precisely because it has allowed us to develop generic propositions that really do help us understand better, why and how a species might come into being. We not only have the capacity to theorize about our primate heritage, we can usefully locate and organize our ancestors. The conception of fixed kinds from the beginning of time cannot help at all, because it denies that coming to be is possible. Here is another example: The understanding of the social context of Elizabethan life better helps us to understand Shakespeare's writing of *Hamlet* than Freud's *Oedipal Complex*.

This former conception does more for us, allowing us to generate more and better generic propositions, than the latter. From a study of the social context, we can determine what education Shakespeare might have had, what influences were prominent, and what the general intellectual milieu was. The latter conception gives us very little leeway in the manner of anticipated consequences, because it restricts our investigation to a predetermined understanding of the play. Such a conception can only arise after a thorough examination of the context has taken place.

Once inquiry has established a set of anticipated consequences and successfully shown that these are the fact of the matter for an inquirer or inquirers, it is tested by others. Until this testing occurs, the anticipated consequences are merely hypotheses. Frequent testing of inquiry over lengthy spans of time tends to generate common sense facts of the matter. The existential import of inquiry is played up, and the manner in which inquiry arrived at the conclusions it did, are played down. Often, common sense is habituated: we develop a stock of habits that we use in solving day-to-day problems and in our interactions with others. We have and use the dispositions to treat certain situations in a certain way, and, for the most part, we are successful. What distinguishes scientific inquiry from common sense is the role of ideas. Scientific inquiry operates largely at the level of abstract reasoning and ideas: common sense operates at the level of the concrete (LW 13 1938, p. 119).

What of the self-corrective aspect? How does inquiry adjust in situations wherein anticipated consequences don't pan out? It is helpful to see inquiry as loosely circular, or spiral, here. Inquiry begins and ends in situations. Indeterminate and (later) problematic situations are the beginnings of an inquiry: A satisfactory situation is the end of an inquiry. An inquiry then, is a whole with its beginnings and endings in a situation. What occurs between the beginning and the end is adjustment. We make adjustments to our judgment of what constitutes the problem; we make adjustments to our conceptions and generic propositions; we make adjustments in the way we modify the environment and the tools we use to do so. What counts as a successful inquiry is a satisfactory or settled situation, and until this is accomplished, inquiry self-corrects. If I am having difficulty understanding a passage in a text, I need to identify the specific problem, develop anticipated routes to successful understanding, and evaluate these. I also need to evaluate the methods I am using to help me understanding the text. If, for example, I am using a set of techniques that are unhelpful (I am reading the passage over and over again, with no better understanding taking place), then I need to change or develop new methods. My generic proposition; I will read and read again until understanding take place, is faulty. Perhaps I need to consult a dictionary of Elizabethan terms.

Universal conceptions and general propositions self-correct. A conception is only as good as the meaningful relations it generates. If it doesn't hook together well with other meanings and other ideas, then it probably isn't very helpful. Beyond this, conceptions have their operational nature bound up in the generic propositions that evolve from them. If the generic propositions don't pan out; if the proposition, that I should do this to obtain this or that effect, does not succeed, either the generic proposition itself is faulty, or the conception that instantiates the proposition is. Repeated failures of a generic proposition should alert the inquirer to the strong possibility that the original conception is faulty. This necessitates returning to the problem in question, reframing it, and developing new conceptions and anticipated consequences.

CONFLICTS AND DOUBTS REGARDING INQUIRY

Despite the self-correcting nature of inquiry, many who have read Dewey have and continue to have doubts regarding the overall plausibility of the theory. The first concern is that Dewey leaves little room for emotion and imagination in his theory of inquiry.[4] The criticism boils down to the fact that experimentation, rather than the affective traits of humans, dictates what will count as a successful inquiry. A related concern is that inquiry denigrates or downplays, abstract thinking.[5] Many critics of progressive education latch onto this as the central reason for the demise of American education. Finally, there is the concern that the self-correcting nature of inquiry is too lenient on what counts as hard facts and truths: that facts of the matter have more force and depth than Dewey's theory of inquiry gives credit for.[6] I discuss each of these in turn.

The first concern that Dewey leaves little room for emotion and imagination in his theory of inquiry has generated a number of sophisticated responses. One has been to play up the aesthetic and qualitative nature of inquiry, particular in contexts of art. Here what is important is the satisfaction of the experience rather than the particular techniques and methods. What inquiry aims for; the unified whole, is what is given priority. Another has been to stress Dewey's notion of deliberative rehearsal—a notion he develops in *How We Think* (LW 8 1933, p. 187–88). Here, one of the central features of inquiry is to imagine anticipated consequences to the tentative solutions to the problem at hand. Yet another has been to suggest that inquiry does not separate emotion and imagination from the contexts in which they occur: rather, it orders and controls responses so that richer and more deeply felt emotions could surface. Only on a dichotomous approach to inquiry, where hard facts are stressed to the detriment of other traits, is the denigration of imagination and emotion a problem. All of these solutions are correct.

The second concern, that Dewey downplays abstract thinking, is easily dealt with once we realize that conceptions are required for the various existential propositions to function. What authors are usually getting at when they criticize Dewey for denigrating abstract thought, though, is the tentative nature that Dewey assigns conceptions and propositions; the abstract thoughts that Dewey supposedly endorses are tentative because they are dependent on their operational status. The abstract thoughts that these critics have in mind are often timeless truths or metaphysical states of affairs. They endorse just what Dewey does not: a realm of fixed ideas or notions. Rather than begging the question of who is right, those who are metaphysically inclined towards fixed truths, absolute principles or laws, and certainty regarding the findings of science and knowledge, will not be satisfied by any response Dewey's theory of inquiry might provide. Likewise, proponents of Dewey's theory of inquiry will always be suspicious of attempts to fix, once and for all, ideas, notions, and concepts.

The third concern is Dewey's supposed lack of ability to pronounce on hard facts or truths of the matter. This is correct. What counts as truth for Dewey is very different from a correspondence theory of truth common to early Enlightenment thinkers and early twentieth-century empiricists. Dewey prefers the term "warranted assertibility" over truth, because truth contains too much baggage for us to be able to work with it satisfactorily (LW 13 1938, pp. 15, 17). The settled results of inquiry (and this includes conceptions and propositions) are always potentially subject to modification or even outright dismissal. When we point to the world and say that does not change or that is the fact of the matter, Dewey would agree with us. But this does not change the point Dewey is making, that facts of the matter are potentially subject to change under varied conditions, and these conditions are occasioned by the problems we face. Nevertheless, this does not change the fact that to hold something as tentative, rather than for all time, is not, despite some critics' concerns, to put the world in peril, at least, not all at once, as William James famously opined.

CONCLUSION

Let us put it all together. Inquiry begins with an indeterminate situation. An indeterminate situation is unsettling, as Dewey maintains. Active investigation into an indeterminate situation begins and a judgment that this constitutes a genuine problem follows. The development of anticipatory consequences, that portend a satisfying solution, is undertaken. This involves two sorts of ideas. The first is conceptions. These are often abstract, and only indirectly relate to the existential traits that fulfill the requirements of a satisfactory solution. They have their worth in how well they relate to other ideas, and how well they produce newer and better meanings and general propositions. The other sort of idea is a generic or existential proposition. These tell us what will happen when we act. If our conceptions are correct, these propositions will often bear fruit. If not, we may need to devise new generic propositions, or revise our conceptions. The aim in all of this is to reach a settled, determinate situation—a satisfying solution to the problem at hand.

CHAPTER TWO

Inquiry in Science Education

When we speak of inquiry in science education, we speak of inquiry in contexts that involve active experimentation with phenomena, collection of data, formation of hypotheses, consideration of theories and laws; and evaluation of results, often involving, but not limited to, laboratory work. Rough examples of science education include the familiar experiments in chemistry and physics; the cultivation of living organisms (biology); the observations of changes in weather (geography and meteorology); the collection of flora and fauna (biology and natural history); the dissection and examination of tissues and organs; and the evaluation of rocks for lines of cleavage (geology), et cetera. Science education cuts across all of these. Indeed, there is even good reason to blur the distinction between science education and the education of art and music, as these contexts also use experimental techniques and active manipulation of phenomena in their own right. What makes science scientific is not the subject matter or content, it is the methods, techniques, and attitudes and tempers, working together to solve a specified problem to a satisfactory conclusion. Nevertheless, science education, which has long connoted the sort of inquiry that takes place in the laboratory, belongs to the disciplines of biology, chemistry, geology, and physics; although this state of affairs is more a result of tradition than reasoned argument.

WHAT DOES INQUIRY IN SCIENCE EDUCATION CONSIST OF?

What distinguishes inquiry in science education (and science generally) is, first of all, the variety of techniques utilized, the formalization and communication of meanings in symbols, the establishment of theories and laws, and the ongoing attempts at the reproduction and falsification of results. Science tries to repeat results in differing contexts, for differing situations. Success occurs when these attempts solve the problem at hand. Success only lasts as long as the conclusions of the research stand their ground; that is, they are not falsifiable. If they are falsified, they no longer accord the distinction of being right or true.

As well, inquiry in science education is often at an abstract level, and much of the work is done at the level of conception. This is particularly true for theoretical sciences such as quantum mechanics, particle physics, wave physics, physical chemistry, astrophysics, biological and biogeographic modelling, and population ecology and epidemiology. Inquiry in science education actively exploits these characteristics for the pedagogical purposes of helping a student master good habits of inquiring. These habits, once formed, are used in the production of further, more specialized habits. Eventually, a stock of habits is built up that becomes second nature to the budding scientist or experimenter.

We have, then, four features that roughly distinguish inquiry in science and science education from inquiry in other contexts. These are:

1. The kinds of techniques utilized.

2. The focus on the establishment of theories and laws.

3. The symbolic formalization and communication of meanings (mathematics and formal logic).

4. The ongoing evaluation of settled results.

Let's take each of these and discuss them more thoroughly. I begin with the techniques of induction and deduction. In *Logic: the Theory of Inquiry*, Dewey tells us that:

> Whatever else the scientific method is or is not, it is concerned with ascertaining the conjunctions of characteristic traits which descriptively determine kinds in relation to one another and the interrelations of characters which constitute abstract conceptions of wide applicability . . . The methods by which generalizations are arrived at have received the name "induction"; the methods by which already existing generalizations are employed have received the name "deduction. . . ." Any account of scientific method must be capable of offering a coherent doctrine of the nature of induction and deduction and of their relations to one another, and the doctrine must accord with what takes place in actual scientific practice. (LW 13 1986, p. 414)

Induction is the means by which we generalize. For example, when we say, I predict that Jessica will do poorly on her final exams, or according to established studies, the likelihood of children from lower socioeconomic statuses graduating from university is lower than the mean, and it is likely that this trend will continue in the future, unless we alter these conditions, we are generalizing. Deduction, by contrast, takes the conclusions of generalizations and makes inferences about what must be the case. If Jack does poorly on his final exams, and all children doing poorly on their final exams have an opportunity for remediation, then Jack, too, has an opportunity for remediation. Likewise, if all children adversely affected by low socioeconomic status are eligible for after-school tutoring, and Sarah is adversely affected by low socioeconomic status, she, too, is eligible for after-school tutoring.

Beginning with Aristotle, science has privileged deduction over induction. Indeed, deduction was the focus of syllogistic logic—the dominant logic of Western thought until the nineteenth century. Syllogistic logic is the kind of logic we discussed in chapter 1 (John and his opposable thumbs). Clearly, this technique has a great legacy. However, as Dewey says, it is often decontextualized and placed in a realm of its own. When this happens, it loses its operational effectiveness. Dewey's aim is to place induction and deduction back into their proper context—that of active experimentation.

> Historically, Induction is a 'psychological process,' or perhaps a 'pedagogical process,' in which certain select persons in whom the potentiality of reason is brought to actuality by means of the forms that are implicit in objects of experience, are led up to or *induced* to apprehend universals which have been necessarily involved all the time in sense qualities and objections of empirical perception. (LW 13 1986, p. 419)

This has been the case throughout much of (educational) history, but this is a false understanding of induction: indeed, Dewey claims that this understanding of induction is an obstacle to inquiry (LW 13 1986, p. 421). Induction is looked upon by Dewey as a phase of inquiry, a phase in which

> the complex of experimental operations by which antecedently existing conditions are so modified that data are obtained which indicate and test proposed modes of solution . . . Any suggested or indicated mode of solutions must be formulated as a *possibility*. (LW 13 1986, p. 423)

Here, Dewey says, what we have done previously in the way of experimentation, obtaining results, et cetera, bears on what we are to do now. The phase of induction terminates in the hypothesis generated. This takes the form, as we have discussed, of an if-then statement. Universal conceptions are hypothesis statements of the kinds: If this is a kidney then a ureter will be found attached to it, leading down to a bladder. If this is pure sodium, when I drop H_2O on it, a violent reaction will occur. If this incline has been greased, I will calculate a reduction in the object's resistance through a noted increase in velocity.

We begin then, with antecedent existing conditions; the facts of the matter that we already have and know. We modify these conditions (drop H_2O on sodium; dissect a fetal pig; run an object across a track) to obtain data which we then place against proposed modes of solution to the problem (which is the kidney? What happens when pure sodium and H_2O come in contact? Does decreasing resistance really increase velocity?). This solution is in the form of an if-then statement or universal conception. But there is more, for induction does not operate in isolation. There is, as Dewey says, "a functional correspondence" between induction and deduction (LW 13 1986, p. 423). In other words, these two operate in tandem.

> The propositions which formulate data must, to satisfy the conditions of inquiry, be such as to determine a problem in the form that indicates a possible solution, while the hypothesis in which the latter is formulated must be such as operationally to provide the new data that fill out and order those previously obtained. There is a continued to-and-fro movement between the set of existential propositions about data and the non-existential propositions about related conceptions. (LW 13 1986, p. 423)

Let us be clear about what counts as induction and what counts as deduction. An if-then proposition is a claim about what does and/or will happen with regards to a situation; an existential state of affairs, and depends on other, particular propositions for it to be tested out. For example: If I drop this H_2O onto pure sodium, a violent reaction will occur. I will now drop some water on this sodium. If I shake this can of Coke and open it, the disturbed gases inside will force the liquid out. Let's shake this can of Coke. If I cut into the retro-abdominal area of this fetal pig, I am more likely to spot the kidney than if I cut into the upper abdomen. Let's get busy dissecting.

These are existential propositions, followed by further, particular propositions that tell us how to act. Both of these propositions, though, rely on abstract conceptions that can only be related and tested deductively. We need abstract conceptions in order to regulate existential propositions. Deduction tests our abstract concepts. Abstract concepts are tested in two ways: the first is how well they hang together with one another. The second is how well they generate existential propositions that are in turn operationalized. What sort of abstract concepts are there? Consider the three examples above. I need the concept of reaction for the first one. This allows me to make sense of the demonstrable changes in weight, volume, heat-energy, et cetera, that are the results of my action. Reaction is the abstract concept. I need the concept of a law (Henry's law) that tells me under what conditions a gas under pressure is subject to expansion and subsequent release in a confined space. Henry's law is the abstract concept. I need the concept of an organ (how it is composed, why it is necessary, what it does; what its relation is to the organism as a whole) to make sense of kidney. The organ is the abstract concept. In other words, I need concepts to represent, to myself and others doing active experimentation, just what it is that holds all of these relations together. Without these, I cannot communicate my findings to others, and I cannot generate existential propositions. I cannot do these because I have no idea of why, where, and what I am doing, or how to go about organizing the many phenomena, findings, and characteristics.

Some conceptions are simple and concrete. Certain customary behaviours are merely rules of thumb, telling us to do this or that in order to obtain certain results. We might call these conventions. These, properly speaking, are generally not the sort of concepts that can accommodate rigorous hypotheses testing. The sorts that do accommodate scrutiny when they are built up and have their meanings "developed in ordered discourse, observation and assemblage of data . . ." are theories (LW 13 1986, p. 428). Theories are clusters of hypotheses brought together in a communicable, meaningful manner. When we make a claim that something will happen when an object is manipulated, or a change in the situation occurs, we are making a hypothesis. Gathering a number of hypotheses together and making a general claim about what is going on in this or that situation is to construct a theory. Analogously, theories act as an edifice, housing various hypotheses built up through active experimentation. Theories rely both on specific, universal conceptions and existential propositions.

Consider the theory of evolution. If we were to take it apart, we would find many subconceptions (genes; species; natural selection; phenotypes, etc.), as well as universal propositions (new species evolve that are better able to transact with their environment; competition for resources favouring the successful, etc.). All of these subconceptions in turn were generated in hypotheses. The theory is parasitic on these universal propositions, but these propositions are dependent on the theory to make sense of what we are doing. Likewise, these universal propositions have their function and force in the particular existential propositions formulated to effect a transformation in the environment. If there are no conceptions or theories, there is no making sense of existential propositions. Likewise, if there are no functioning existential propositions, then there are no functioning conceptions or theories. Universal propositions hang on the ability of specific or particular propositions to be operationalized, and particular propositions derive their raison d'être from universal ones.

Laws establish regularities of *occurrences* such that we can safely establish a causal connection between phenomena under certain conditions. (We wouldn't normally expect to worry about Henry's Law, for example, unless we happened to go scuba diving and subsequently hopped on a plane, or were confronted with a grinning child pointing a shaken can of soda at us). But these conditions can change and with the conditions, the law as well. Causation, the claim that there are necessary connections between phenomena, denotes a function: "the functional relation (correspondence) of the two logical types of propositions" (LW 13 1986, p. 439). Causation means that a certain type of relation, between two different types of propositions, is in effect. But laws are not absolute regularities, forever fixed and operating in every circumstance.

> The fallacy vitiating the view that scientific laws are formulations of uniform unconditioned sequences of change arises from taking the function of the universal [if-then] proposition as if it were part of the structural content of the existential [particular] propositions. (LW 13 1986, p. 439)

It is true that sequential linkage of changes (a casual chain) is the gold standard of the scientific method, but this is just to say that under condition X, we can be as certain as we possibly can that Y will occur. Alternatively, if Jasmine forgets her schoolbooks, then she will be unable to complete her project. This causal proposition is itself a proposition that requires continuous testing.

The other method common to most scientific inquiries is mathematics. Mathematics, like logic, is a tool. It has its genesis in the havings and doings of experiences. Dewey tells us that:

> Historically, the operations by which symbol-meanings are transformed were first borrowed from and closely allied to physical operations; in gross, in such words as deliberation, pondering, reflection, and more specifically in counting and calculation. As meanings were modified to satisfy the conditions imposed by membership in an interrelated system, operations were also modified to meet the requirements of the new conceptual material. Operations became as abstract as the materials to which they apply and hence of a character expressed, and capable only of expression, in a new order of symbols. (LW 13 1986, p. 392)

Mathematics and formal logic are concerned only with their relations. They do not participate directly in existential contexts. They are abstract in the sense that they relate to each other, as meanings, and not to something beyond or outside.

> When, however, discourse is conducted exclusively with refer-
> ence to satisfaction of its own logical conditions, or, as we say,
> for its own sake, the subject-matter is not only nonexistential
> in immediate reference but is itself formed on the ground of
> freedom from existential reference of even the most indirect,
> delayed and ulterior kind. It is then mathematical. The subject-
> matter is completely abstract and formal because of its complete
> freedom from the conditions imposed upon conceptual material
> which is framed with reference to final existential application.
> Complete freedom and complete abstractness are here synonymous
> terms. . . . Change in the context of inquiry effects a change in
> its intent and contents. Physical conceptions differ from those
> of common sense. For their context is not that of use-enjoyment
> but is that of institution of conditions of systematic extensive
> inference. A further new context is provided when all reference
> to existential applicability is eliminated. The result is not simply
> a higher degree of abstractness, but a new order of abstractions,
> one that is instituted and controlled only by the category of
> abstract relationship. The necessity of transformation of mean-
> ings in discourse in order to determine warranted existential
> propositions provides, nevertheless, the connecting link with the
> general pattern of inquiry. (LW 13 1986, p. 393)

Here Dewey distinguishes between two types of universal propositions. On the one hand, we have propositions of physical laws. These are universal hypothetical propositions such as the laws of gravitation or of motion. These physical laws are "framed with reference to the possibility of ultimate exis-tential application, the contents are affected by that intent" (LW 13 1986, pp. 394–95). On the other hand, there are mathematical propositions or mathematical laws that have no relationship to existential considerations (LW 13 1986, p. 395). What distinguishes these? The answer is the contexts they arise in and the uses to which they are put. A physical law certainly uses mathematics. But that is precisely the point: mathematics is used (think of force as mass times acceleration and multiplication as the technique involved). But multiplication for its own sake, in support of no physical law, is by virtue of its freedom from other contexts,

> free from the conditions that require any limited interpreta-
> tion. They [mathematical propositions] have no meaning or

interpretation save that which is formally imposed by the need
of satisfying the condition of transformability within the system
[of mathematics], with no extrasystemic reference whatsoever.
(LW 13 1986, p. 395)

In sum, the meanings mathematical propositions generate in the context of
mathematics alone are to and for, one another.

One might conclude that mathematics has little or nothing to do with
the existential contexts of inquiry, but this would be hasty: mathematics
indirectly informs existential propositions and is influenced by them, in
turn. Dewey's last line about mathematical propositions being to and for
one another does not discount the importance of mathematics to existential situations. For example, number relates to number, measure relates to
measure, and line relates to line. These in turn, though, do relate to situations indirectly. Measures, numbers, and other results of mathematics often
occur in existential situations for existential situations, and although one
number has its direct relation with another, these numbers gain meaning
and use in the context of the situation under investigation. They tell us
what is likely to happen when we try to manipulate the environment or
the traits of a situation in one way rather than another. They tell us what
to look for in the way of success or failure. They help us locate and gauge
our anticipated results of inquiry.

WHAT CONTEXTS DOES
INQUIRY IN SCIENCE EDUCATION OPERATE IN?

Traditionally, science education includes laboratory experimentation. However, there are other less familiar contexts in which science operates. The
paradigm of scientific inquiry is interrogation of phenomena in a laboratory
or otherwise highly structured setting, wherein patient, careful attention
to changes is measured. Further changes are anticipated, partly through
theory and mathematical techniques, partly through direct manipulation
of the subject matter, and hypotheses are tested for their consequences.
Accuracy and precision are stressed throughout. A high level of abstraction is often required, particularly at the level of theory. Many attempts at
deliberate falsification of the results ensue (generally by other researchers),
in an effort to determine under what conditions the results can be said to
obtain, and to test the usefulness of the theory generated to explain the
phenomena at hand.

This of course nicely encapsulates physical science. It is less inclusive,
however, of the natural or life sciences, where measurement is often not the

central focus, and what counts as accuracy and precision differ radically from what takes place, say, in a chemistry lab. Moving beyond the life sciences, earth sciences also fits with difficulty into this paradigm of measure, accuracy, and precision. For example, human observation skills may count for more in identifying crystal structures than they may in chemistry, which often rely on mechanical and/or electronic instruments to ascertain changes in phenomena. The social sciences in particular present unique challenges to the model of laboratory science, partly for ideological and political reasons.

Consider what sorts of techniques are necessary for the following three examples:

1. The calculation of the force involved in one object moving at a steady speed and hitting another object.

2. The correct identification of striated columnar epithelium in the smooth muscles of a pig artery.

3. The observation of lines of cleavage in sedimentary rock.

Each of these will require different techniques. At a minimum, the calculation of force in the first example will require an understanding and use of a physical law ($F = MA$), as well as mathematics (multiplication), balls, means of measuring distance, time, and weight of balls, et cetera. For the second example, a microscope is necessary, as is access to a diagram or chart detailing the tissue in question. Here, physical laws are not important: close observation and manual dexterity are. This also goes for the third example. Beyond the tools (chisel) needed to cleave rock, charts or diagrams and keen observation is required. The point is that different contexts, in which different subject-matter is under consideration, necessitate different techniques, different approaches, indeed, different use of (differing) abstract ideas. We do not need to understand the concept of force to dissect an artery and examine its smooth muscle under a microscope. Likewise, we do not need to understand the role of smooth muscle in arterial vasoconstriction and dilation to calculate an object's kinetic energy. We develop different ideas and have recourse to different concepts for the differing contexts of scientific inquiry, all the while holding closely to experimentation. Sometimes, we mistake the physical sciences as the paradigm case of all sciences, and attempt to reduce what takes place in biology or geology to physical or mathematical laws. This is a mistake. Although there may be a role for both in certain biological or geological contexts (population analysis or epidemiology in biology requiring statistical techniques: calculation of stresses in structural geology requiring knowledge of mechanics), these are not exhaustive of what goes on in these contexts.

Scientific inquiry operates wherever active experimentation takes place. This experimentation can be physical, as in physics and chemistry, but it need not be. Active experimentation can take place at the level of conceptions and ideas. Attempting to understand a scientific law is scientific inquiry (or at least, a part of it) when anticipation of consequences takes place. Thought is a central ingredient in scientific inquiry: perhaps the most important ingredient.

HOW DOES INQUIRY IN SCIENCE EDUCATION OPERATE?

Inquiry is context-bound and self-correcting. I have also said that there are techniques, attitudes, and tempers that are time-tested and coalesce to form a general method. We may call this general method the experimental method. This is fundamental for scientific inquiry: without the habits and attitudes of experimentation, there can be, properly speaking, no inquiry let alone scientific inquiry. One of the aims of science education (I believe the central aim) is and ought to be the cultivation of this experimental method through helping the student to develop some of the habits and techniques required of those that do science.

Dewey discusses the operation of inquiry in science education most fully in *Democracy and Education*. But Dewey does so with a caveat: do not begin with the subject-matter in its perfected form (MW 9 1980, p. 228). This is so because it is entirely too abstract, as the focus is on laws and conceptions, rather than existential havings and doings, and organization of phenomena has already taken place, giving students little meaningful hands-on work and even less in the way of anticipated consequences to accomplish. Dewey prefers what he calls the chronological method: "The . . . method which begins with the experience of the learner and [that] develops from that the proper modes of scientific treatment . . ." (MW 9 1980, p. 228). Dewey continues:

> What the pupil learns he at least understands. Moreover, by fol-
> lowing, in connection with problems selected from the material
> of ordinary acquaintance, the methods by which scientific men
> have reached their perfected knowledge, he gains independent
> power to deal with material within his range, and avoids the
> mental confusion and intellectual distaste attendant upon study-
> ing matter whose meaning is only symbolic. Since the mass of
> pupils are never going to become scientific specialists, it is much
> more important that they should get some insight into what sci-
> entific method means than that they should copy at long range

and second hand the results which scientific men have reached (MW 9 1980, pp. 228–29).

Drawing on previous arguments to the effect that children learn best by actively engaging in the world around them, testing materials in various ways, sorting and selecting best practices through trial and error, Dewey recommends a practical approach to science education: work with materials. This is not enough, however. The ends to which materials are to be manipulated must have some connection with the student's life outside the laboratory and classroom: that is, the ends for the student cannot simply be the ends of science for, say, a practicing chemist or field biologist. Genuine problems must be established before active experimentation takes place, and this requires that students, not teachers or textbooks, legitimize what counts as a problem.

The difficulty is, of course, that without exposure to the problems of science, little in the way of what counts as problems comes into the student's purview. Add to this the differences among students with respect to background knowledge, exposure to scientific role models (often a problem for young girls), the quality of previous scientific instruction, et cetera, and the difficulties mount. In many cases, the seemingly most elementary examples and situations must be drawn upon to help students to legitimate scientific problems. This is a daunting task if one is attempting to explain abstract conceptions, such as physical or chemical laws. Nevertheless, it is often necessary.

The other central feature of science education is that it is to be allied with social progress. Science for its own sake is not denigrated; rather, it is subordinated to practical need and desire. Dewey's accounting of the history of scientific development suggests that science for its own sake is a relative latecomer. Let us take the case of mathematics: development of abstract mathematics and formal logic, for example, did not fully occur until the nineteenth century. What science has accomplished historically is technology. As Dewey puts it:

> The wonderful transformation of production and distribution known as the industrial revolution is the fruit of experimental science. Railways, steamboats, electric motors, telephone and telegraph, automobiles, aeroplanes and dirigibles [and we can add to this list jets, semi-conductors, computer chips, recombinant DNA techniques, genetic engineering, and more ominously, nuclear weapons] are conspicuous evidences of the application of science in life. But none of them would be of much importance without the thousands of less sensational inventions by means of

which natural science has been rendered tributary to our daily life. (MW 9 1980, p. 232)

These technologies, these inventions, are primarily the products of our "pre-existent desires, rather than [having] modified the quality of human purposes" (MW 9 1980, p. 232). But significant, lifesaving devices have obviously been developed, and if we broaden technologies (in keeping with Dewey) to include all artefacts, we are easily led to the conclusion that much, if not most, of our social practices has at least some qualitative value. Dewey wants to take technology further, to ameliorate human suffering and to help solve social problems. Science education should have this as its goal, beyond the development of the habits of scientific inquiry. Indeed, it is not a stretch to say that for Dewey, one of the attitudes of scientific inquiry is the belief in, and desire for, science in the service of human problems.

CONFLICTS AND DOUBTS IN SCIENCE EDUCATION

In both theory and practice, Dewey's notion of science education has been criticized. Historically, there are those fearful that the curriculum will be taken over by scientistic experimenters bent on abandoning nonexperimental subjects such as literature, history, or art, and treating these subjects in an experimental fashion. We see these critics today as well. Often, they lament the damage that has been done either in the name of, or by, Dewey and progressivist education (see also, note 4). Some of these criticisms devolve into further concerns regarding the role of emotion and imagination in experimentation, as I mentioned in the previous chapter. Others concern the subjectivist menace: the menace of scientific inquiry somehow constructing knowledge, as opposed to observing or measuring real effects in the physical world.[7] Yet others are concerned that in the supposedly wholesale turn to experimentation and scientific inquiry, the humanist traditions will be sidelined, with disastrous consequences for (particularly western) civilization.[8] Finally, experimentation of the sort Dewey promotes for science education seems incredibly difficult to undertake because it is time, labor, and intellectually intensive. I take these criticisms up in turn.

The first criticism concerns the dangers of experimental methods in the curriculum and in particular, the damage done by well-meaning but naïve educators in foisting this on students. This issue is often run together with the humanist one: the issue that experimental method can only usher in instrumental, means-end reasoning, but it cannot tell us how or why, to live better lives. Countless critics, educational and otherwise, have made these charges (turn to the footnotes for some striking and famous examples). The best answer to this criticism is to have these critics look at the contexts in which experimentation operates. As I have maintained throughout, inquiry is context-sensitive: it does not reproduce or bring the same techniques, tempers, or outcomes to bear in every context. When we attempt to do so, we often find that inquiry fails, and we have to go back and develop new methods for the situation at hand. What counts as inquiry in science education is not what counts as inquiry in other contexts. Most critics (unwittingly) take inquiry in science to be paradigmatic of all inquiry, but this is to overlook the many cases and places where inquiry simply does not operate this way, and all of this is to be found in Dewey's texts, providing one undertakes a thorough review of these.

The second criticism concerns subjectivism, and in particular, the construction of knowledge. It has become popular to run Dewey's experimental inquiry together with Jean Piaget or Ernst von Glaserfeld's understandings of child development, and contemporary research on the social context of scientific inquiry, and jump to the conclusion that Dewey, too, was a constructivist. But this is a faulty conclusion. Though there are certain similarities between Dewey, Piaget, and the sociological study of science, there are pronounced differences. And it is these differences that are glossed in bringing these together. One central claim of thoroughgoing constructivism contradicts Dewey's theory of knowledge. Far from concluding that the mind, or ideas construct objects or make nature (which is what subjectivism amounts to), Dewey believes that ideas are anticipated consequences, abstractly considered, that then have their operational worth in other ideas and existential propositions that do lead to actual, physical, effects. In other words, there is no argument here that ideas construct the world. Indeed, it would be better to say that the world begins the quest for ideas, though this too ignores the inextricably linked natures of world, experience, and inquiry. I am not saying that all constructivists are subjectivists; rather, I am suggesting we approach Dewey with the qualification that Dewey's inquiry is based in real, existential, and operational propositions derived (in part) from real, existential changes.

The final criticism may be the most difficult to overcome. There is no getting around it: the role of the science educator (inclusive of the math educator) is going to be difficult, time-consuming, and intellectually demanding. Part of the reason is the need to understand and appreciate the developmental stages of students; what is appropriate knowledge for them; what they can and cannot generally accomplish in the classroom, and what manipulables and resources follow from this. This of course is an issue for all teachers, everywhere. But what complicates this is the additional needs to have the child operationalize the abstractions produced and developed in an inquiry. There is a risk inherent in remaining at the level of abstraction and idea. If abstractions and ideas are not operationalized, if existential propositions are not developed out of these, if propositions that can then effect a change in materials are not in place, then follow-through cannot take place, and the reasons why we are making abstractions become shrouded. If a child is unable to form the concept of basic, mathematical operations such as carry over (let us say, he lacks number sense), strategies for enacting this operation when the situation arises, will not be available to that child. One of the difficulties with mathematics is the abstract nature of the subject matter. What makes this a difficulty is the requirement that one work at the level of abstraction constantly, with few or no discernable existential consequences.

Young children cannot work at this level constantly without loss. They need to see the operationalized results of their inquiry, regardless of what context the scientific inquiry takes place in. One time-honored way to overcome this is to have children do less abstract work initially, and as they get older and further ahead in school, to supplement their inquiry with more and further abstraction. This is what Dewey generally recommends, but this is not always the best course to take. And it is particularly difficult with certain disciplines, notably mathematics, where much of the inquiry is abstract from the get-go. Numbers are not tangibles or material, they are symbols. Somehow the teacher has to find a way to stress the abstraction necessary for the child to be able to succeed in the experimentation. The way to do this, Dewey urges, is to allow the child to develop the abstractions herself. Mathematical abstractions, though they are conceptual, are also tools (as with all ideas), and they emerge when we anticipate consequences in the context of real inquiry, using real materials and solving real problems. They do not naturally emerge: we have to work to get at them. But they do emerge if active investigation is undertaken. We might say that ideas suggest themselves to children when they actively consider alternatives that lead to potentially successful strategies, and this should be the focus of the teacher; to have students themselves actively consider these alternatives and play them out as best as possible to see if they are viable.

This demands a great deal of anticipatory work on the part of the teacher. The teacher has to dramatize the inquiry beforehand, play out the potential ideas that would lead to a successful inquiry; be knowledgeable of the ideas that will lead to dead ends; understand what will count as success for her students; and be prepared to guide the students to develop these desired ideas. This anticipatory work, however, is often the sticking point. The realities of educational practice negate much of the teacher's reflective power and hindrances to an environment that would support this (more time between classes; more time to develop lessons; more and better laboratory equipment; less attention to rote, including one size fits all tests) are all too frequent. The greatest impediment to successful scientific inquiry for the vast majority of children is not a child's ability, or a teacher's, for that matter: it is a failure, often worsened by countervailing institutional demands and contradictory goals, to imagine and to create the institutional and classroom contexts (inclusive of small groups) in which scientific inquiry can take hold.

CONCLUSION

Inquiry in science education operates along the lines of general inquiry, beginning with a felt difficulty, an indeterminate situation, followed by problem identification, leading to the development of anticipated consequences that are made formal in hypotheses statements, and that draw on conceptions and ideas, together with tools and techniques, to help measure anticipated changes in phenomena. The tools and techniques are various, and are dependent on the contexts in which the inquiry takes place. The most significant features of scientific inquiry to pay attention to are those of problem-finding and problem-solving, the development of the attitudes necessary for scientific inquiry (accuracy and precision in one's measurements and attention to detail); the focus on abstract conceptions, and the aims and purposes to which scientific inquiry is set.

CHAPTER THREE

Inquiry in Social Science Education

Unlike inquiry in science education, inquiry in social science education encompasses human nature and conduct. The subject matters cut across the disciplines of biology, anthropology, sociology, geography, history, and psychology. Moreover, (perhaps most importantly) social science is closely tied to ethics. Why we behave the way we do to one another, given our specific circumstances, is a question as interesting and important as what the physiologic basis of human behaviour is; both of these questions are the proper subject matter of social science, particularly if the goal of inquiry is to obviate social problems.

This leads us to ask the further question; how ought we to behave to one another? Social sciences for Dewey do not make much of the fact/value distinction, common to natural science; a distinction that imposes a gulf between what we describe as a state of natural affairs (how things really are) and what we choose for ourselves (what we value). Though Dewey does not argue that existing states of social affairs must necessarily lead to desired social or behavioural changes, he does argue that this is the proper point of departure for any intelligent social change. Students inquiring into problems of human conduct or social problems, have opportunities to role-play such intelligent social change as they learn about the accomplishments of past peoples and those in other parts of the world.

WHAT DOES INQUIRY IN
SOCIAL SCIENCE EDUCATION CONSIST OF?

Inquiry in social science is distinguished from inquiry in other contexts because of its direct bearing on issues of human conduct; human behaviour is the key ingredient here. It is understood that the contexts in which human behavior is studied are very different from the contexts in which the physical

41

universe or even flora and fauna, is studied. Nevertheless, as Dewey maintains throughout his vast work, this does not allow the social sciences or social scientists to abrogate their responsibilities to engage in rigorous experimental inquiry. Indeed, as Dewey saw it, the greatest impediment to the problems of human conduct in our time was the backwardness of the social sciences in relation to the physical sciences. Having the social sciences catch up was a central characteristic of all Dewey's writings on the topic. Not surprisingly, Dewey thought education must play a central role in this.

Beyond the study of human behavior and conduct, social sciences demand an inquiry that has special techniques and attributes of its own. In contrast to the physical sciences, the general warrants or laws of social science are less easy to come by. Interpretation plays a great role in understanding human behaviour. Methods such as observation, interviews, and performative analyses, take on much greater weight in many cases. Beyond this, sensitivity to the plight of suffering is necessary, so that empathy may be fostered—to understand and act on—the behaviours of others. Most importantly there is the normative question that lies behind all social scientific research: what are we to do with the results? The answers do not come on the face of the results of social scientific inquiry: they have to be deliberated upon. And this brings social science straight into the territory of ethics and politics.

We have four characteristics that distinguish social science from other modes of inquiry. These are:

1. The environment in which social science research takes place; the environment of human interaction and conduct.

2. The subject-matter under investigation: human beings.

3. The techniques and attributes of inquiry common to social sciences—observations, interviews, performative analyses, and interpretation of findings.

4. The normative claims often made on the basis of the findings of social science.

Let's take each of these other distinctions and discuss them thoroughly. The subject-matter of the social sciences is manifestly different than in the natural sciences, but this need not force us to the conclusion that social cannot mean experimental. Dewey tells us that:

> The question is not whether the subject-matter of human relations is or can ever become a science in the sense in which physics is now a science, but whether it is such as to permit of

the development of methods which, as far as they go, satisfy the
logical conditions that have to be satisfied in other branches of
inquiry. (LW 13 1986, p. 481)

Here is the crux of the matter: the subject under investigation is not what
is at issue with regards to the difficulty of the science of social relations:
what is at issue are the methods that in turn allow for the logical conditions
to be as rigorously developed and expressed, as in the natural or physical
sciences. This is not to say that the subject matter is somehow transparent
to the researcher; indeed, this is most obviously not the case. Rather, the
social scientist must work as hard, and probably harder, than her corresponding colleague in the natural or physical sciences, to produce the rigorous,
logically consistent findings demanded of all science.

Dewey reminds us first of all, that inquiry, regardless of its nature,
takes place in the context of social relations (LW 13 1986, p. 481). I have
more to say about this, but for now, I want to clear up confusion regarding
the ease with which we inquire into various subject matters. I note that
even the natural and physical sciences are, to varying degrees, opaque. The
assumption that the subject-matters of the natural and physical sciences
are transparent, or reveal themselves more easily than the subject-matters
of the social sciences, is false. It is the case that physical inquiry is more
restricted, as Dewey says, in its scope. But this is not the same as saying
that it is transparent. Indeed, the issue is not how to get human relations
into a pattern that makes it easier to identify causal regularities; rather, it
is to develop the methods and techniques to arrive at logically consistent
propositions, conceptions, and theories to solve human problems. The task
of inquiring is not merely descriptive in social science; it is interpretive and
normative. As Dewey says:

> The conclusion that agreement of activities and their conse-
> quences is a test and a moving force in scientific advance is in
> harmony with the position that the ultimate end and test of all
> inquiry is the transformation of a problematic situation (which
> involves confusion and conflict) into a unified one. That it is
> much more difficult to accomplish this end in social inquiry
> than in the restricted field of physical inquiry is a fact. But it is
> not a fact which constitutes an inherent logical or theoretical
> difference between the two kinds of inquiry. On the contrary,
> the presence of practical difficulties should operate, as within
> physical inquiry itself, as an intellectual stimulus and challenge
> to further application. (LW 13 1986, pp. 484–85)

One of the interesting conclusions Dewey draws is that there is no gap between the social, natural, and physical sciences inhibiting these from contributing to one another. There is a gap, of course, but it is functional. Indeed, Dewey goes as far as to say that the social sciences require the findings and the inquiry of the natural and physical sciences. "The theoretical bearing of this consideration [of the interaction of phenomena] is that social phenomena cannot be understood except as there is prior understanding of physical conditions and the laws of their interactions" (LW 13 1986, p. 486).

It is this, Dewey says, that

> accounts in part for the retarded and immature state of social subjects. Only recently has there been sufficient understanding of physical relations . . . to provide the necessary intellectual instrumentalities for effective intellectual attack upon social phenomena. Without physical knowledge there are no means of analytic resolution of complex and grossly macroscopic social phenomena into simpler forms. (LW 13 1986, p. 414)

It is tempting to conclude that Dewey makes a case for the reduction of social-scientific phenomena to physical phenomena. That is to say, that Dewey thinks all social-scientific phenomena is ultimately of the same kind as physical phenomena. However, this would be a mistake. Dewey is not saying this. He is saying that social sciences will remain underdeveloped until we accept that our social world contains within itself, the physical and natural world, and that separating the two off from one another, while an obvious move, is misleading. As brute states of affairs, the natural and physical world and social interaction run together. The lesson is to realize that methods and techniques must take this fact of the matter into account.

Techniques and methods of the social sciences follow from the unique nature of the subject matter and the problems. Most obviously, understanding human relations requires distinct techniques and methods to glean useful information—techniques that would be inappropriate in other contexts. But some techniques cut across the divide. This is the case with observation. Observation reports, for example; reports on what we see or measure may seem to be solid and reliable, as is the case in the natural and physical sciences. This assumption, however, is mistaken.

> The assumption that social inquiry is scientific if proper techniques of observation and record (preferably statistical) are employed (the standard of propriety being set by borrowing from techniques used in physical sciences) . . . fails to observe the logical conditions which in physical science give the techniques of observing and

measuring their standing and force. This point will be developed by considering the idea, which is current, that social inquiry is scientific only when complete renunciation of any reference to *practical* affairs is made its precondition. (LW 13 1986, p. 492)

Indeed, quantifying social-scientific data is often inappropriate. This is so because the results obtained bear little resemblance to the existential situation at hand. The situation is what is investigated, not the measurement of this or that aspect of it. Measurement aids us in coming to understand a situation. However, measurement can only be significant in the context of the situation itself. It cannot mean anything beyond this. To take a measure as any more significant than as a tool to help us make sense of the total situation, is to mistake the part (the measure) for the whole (the situation) with disastrous results for the outcome of inquiry.

> The connection of social inquiry, as to social data and as to conceptual generalizations, with practice is intrinsic not external. Any problem of scientific inquiry that does not grow out of actual (or 'practical') social conditions is factitious; it is arbitrarily set by the inquirer instead of being objectively produced and controlled. All the techniques of observation employed in the advanced sciences may be conformed to, including the use of the best statistical methods to calculate probable errors, etc., and yet the material ascertained be scientifically 'dead,' i.e., irrelevant to a genuine issue, so that concern with it is hardly more than a form of intellectual busy work. (LW 13 1986, p. 492–93)

This begs the question, though: just what are the techniques and methods of the social sciences? Social science occurs when the mode of observation discriminates adverse and favourable conditions in an existing situation involving human conduct, or what works better in terms of the anticipated end from what does not (LW 13 1986, p. 493). This is inclusive of the concerns of value. This is not unlike the situation in the natural and physical sciences, in which ends in view are also proposed and tested. However, what is different is the contingent nature of the proposals, the contingent nature of the propositions and conceptions proffered, the difference in what counts as a test, and the contingent nature of the settled results (LW 13 1986, p. 494–95). Judgments certainly are made in social-scientific contexts; judgments that have evaluative force. However, these judgments, and the propositions developed to test them, are intrinsic to the subject matter under investigation. What we do about these states of affairs requires deliberation.

Likewise, principles, laws, and theories are contingent. These have their worth in the solution to the problem or situation at hand. They do not always or often function for problems or contexts beyond the one investigated. The difference between the laws, principles, and theories of the natural and physical sciences and the same of the social sciences is not that one is absolutely binding and the other not. This would be to miss the point. Rather, it is that we have had much more success developing and testing natural and physical laws, principles, and theories than we have had developing and testing principles and theories in the social sciences. The laws, principles, and theories of the physical universe that we develop work better in these contexts than those of the social sciences do in theirs because we have worked more vigilantly on these.

As I mentioned earlier, normative or value claims are internal to social-scientific inquiry. This is because the sorts of problems that social science deals with are problems involving human conduct; problems that is, of value. Value here is synonymous with worthwhile, helpful, better, desired, while value-less is synonymous with unhelpful, worse, and undesirable. The idea here is that a judgment of valuation is a judgment that something is useful or helpful in a particular situation, and that the business of social science is to find out what that helpful or useful practice is. Many of the problems that social science has faced come from neglect of this point. As with scientistic accounts of human conduct, traditional moral theories of what is right and good, and bad and evil, have blocked the possibility that an experimental approach to solving problems of social science could occur.

> One of the many obstructions in the way of satisfying the logical conditions of scientific method should receive special notice. Serious social troubles tend to be interpreted in moral terms. That the situations themselves are profoundly moral in their causes and consequences, in the genuine sense of moral, need not be denied. But conversion of the situations investigated into definite problems, that can be intelligently dealt with, demands objective intellectual formation of conditions; and as such a formulation demands in turn complete abstraction from the qualities of sin and righteousness . . . Approach to human problems in terms of moral blame and moral approbation, of wickedness or righteousness, is probably the greatest single obstacle now existing to development of competent methods in the field of social subject-matter. (LW 13 1986, p. 488–89)

The sorts of normative claims made on behalf of social science are not of the good/evil or right/wrong, kinds. To make these sorts of judgments in the context of social science is to entertain moral absolutism. They are rather of the helpful or unhelpful or better or worse, kinds. The point is to solve the problem at hand, not to pass an absolute moral judgment on those that are engaged in a particular activity. Social science is not in the business of making moral pronouncements; it is in the business of solving human problems. Not surprisingly, the task of education with respect to the social sciences is the same.

WHAT CONTEXTS DOES INQUIRY IN
SOCIAL SCIENCE EDUCATION OPERATE IN?

Social scientists operate in the context of human relations and interactions. Social science educators also operate in the context of human relations and interactions, but often at one remove. Consider the differences between a chemistry teacher on the one hand, and a geography teacher on the other. The chemistry teacher helps students conduct experiments on liquids, solids, and gases, and measure the anticipated changes using various methods of analysis, and codify the results in a polished laboratory report. The point being that there is hands-on activity—active experimentation—going on here. Too often, however, social sciences such as geography and history are taught from a textbook or other resource at one remove from an existential situation when active experimentation should be undertaken. To understand human conduct fully, one must be in the midst of human conduct. Unfortunately, this does not take place often enough in the classroom.

One reason given as to why this is the case is that social sciences, unlike physical sciences, require time, opportunities, and funding that is not available. For example, to adequately study human relations in geography classrooms requires more than simply textbook access to the peoples in question, and this is a very difficult if not impossible condition to obtain. In addition, the methods of (physical) geographers often involve global positioning, remote sensing, aerial photography, computer modelling, and other practices not easily teachable. In the case of history, firsthand or archival material is often not available for students to study; thus the turn to textbooks with the results ready-made for the students. The contexts necessary to practice social science and the means to do so, then, are unavailable to students. Or so it is said.

In fact, this does not have to be the case. While it may be true that students cannot access archival material easily, and cannot participate directly in aerial photography, there is much that students can do. Part of the problem is the way we cut the disciplines up: we often see science as whatever is done in a science classroom; this accords with the self-understandings of the scientific disciplines: likewise for the social sciences. When we do this, however, we artificially limit our possibilities for active experimentation. There is little opportunity to cross the borders. This is to forget an important point that Dewey continuously raises when dealing with science education:

> All information and systematized scientific subject matter have been worked out under the conditions of social life and have been transmitted by social means. But this does not prove that all is of equal value for the purposes of forming the disposition and sup-plying the equipment of members of present society. The scheme of a curriculum must take account of the adaptation of studies to the needs of the existing community life; it must select with the intention of improving the life we live in common so that the future shall be better than the past. . . . The things which are social are most fundamental, that is, which have to do with the experiences in which the widest groups share, are the essentials . . . There is truth in the saying that education must first be human and only after than professional." (MW 9 1980, p. 201)

Rather than attempting the construction of an artificial context for the education of the social sciences, it is far more helpful to understand the social-scientific aspects of existing contexts. For example, why would a people need to invent algebra? Why would we want to know how to count? How could understanding that hot air rises be useful to a society? How would a past civilization use levers? What can be gained by understanding other nations' agricultural practices? These are valuable questions to ask, and stu-dents can learn a great deal from attempting to answer them. Rather than clinging to the dichotomy of fact and value, the dichotomy in which facts are treated separately from their usage, social scientific education roots out the value-laden aspects of physical and natural sciences and places these in relief. Social science education is premised on just this: It is not the body of knowledge common to the social sciences that is 'taught'; it is the existential situations of people in all of their manifestations, which are investigated.

Dewey speaks highly of history and geography in *Democracy and Education*.

> The meanings with which activities become charged, concern nature and man. This is an obvious truism, which however, gains meaning when translated into educational equivalents. So translated, it signifies that geography and history supply subject matter which gives background and outlook, intellectual per-

spective, to what might otherwise be narrow personal actions or mere forms of technical skill. With every increase of ability to place our own doings in their time and space connections, our doings gain in significant content. We realize that we are citizens of no mean city in discovering the scene in space of which we are denizens, and the continuous manifestation of endeavour in time of which we are heirs and continuers. Thus our ordinary daily experiences cease to be the things of the moment and gain enduring substance. (MW 9 1980, p. 216)

Consider the following examples:

1. A geography teacher discusses various farming techniques on arable land in ancient Mesopotamia.

2. A history teacher discusses the American Cold War reaction to the Soviet launching Sputnik.

3. A social studies teacher discusses trading practices among Native Americans and Europeans in sixteenth-century North America.

What of each of these ordinary experiences gains substance? The discussion of farming techniques tells us a great deal about how ancient Mesopotamian civilizations subsisted; this information has, and may continue to, help us in our present struggle to feed the world's populations. The sciences these civilizations developed out of farming may thus be helpful to us in our day and age. If possible, the opportunity to farm a patch of arable land in similar weather would go a long way to 'authenticating' the experience. The discussion of the Cold War reaction helps us not only understand what was at stake in the development of technology in the 1950s, but how we responded to world-historical events and how we continue to do so. We gain not only an appreciation of life in the fur trade, but a foreshadowing of the gains and losses that then led to our current relationships with Native Americans and the offspring of European settlers. The point is that geography and history, if the proper connections are made, are invaluable studies for how our present situations have been informed by past ones, how we have created and solved, past 'problems of men,' and how we may yet be able to solve our own.

Dewey thinks history is valuable in (at least) three respects. The first of these is to highlight the industrial nature of life.

Primitive history suggests industrial history. For one of the chief reasons for going to more primitive conditions to resolve the present into more easily perceived factors is that we may realize how the fundamental problems of procuring subsistence, shelter, and protection have been met; and by seeing how these were solved in the earlier days of the human race, form some concep- tions of the long road which has had to be traveled, and of the successive inventions by which the race has been brought forward in culture. We do not need to go into disputes regarding the economic interpretation of history to realize that the industrial history of mankind gives insight into two important phases of social life in a way which no other phase of history can possibly do. It presents us with knowledge of the successive inventions by which theoretical science has been applied to the control of nature in the interests of security and prosperity of social life. It thus reveals the successive causes of social progress. Its other service is to put before us the things that fundamentally concern all men in common—the occupations and values connected with getting a living. (MW 9 1980, p. 223)

The second of these is to highlight the economic nature of life.

Economic history is more human, more democratic, and hence more liberalizing than political history. It deals not with the rise and fall of principalities and powers, but with the growth of the effective liberties, through command of nature, of the common man for who powers and principalities exists. (MW 9 1989, p. 224)

Finally, the third of these is to highlight the intellectual nature of life.

Perhaps the most neglected branch of history in general educa- tion is intellectual history. We are only just beginning to realize that the great heroes who have advanced human destiny are not its politicians, generals, and diplomatists, but the scientific discoverers and inventors who have put into man's hands the instrumentalities of an expanding and controlled experience, and the artists and poets who have celebrated his struggles, triumphs, and defeats in such language . . . that their meaning is rendered universally accessible to others. . . . Surely no better way could be devised of instilling a genuine sense of the part which mind has to play in life than a study of history which makes plain how the entire advance from savagery to civilization has been dependent upon intellectual discoveries and inventions, and the extent to which the things which ordinarily figure most largely

in historical writings have been side issues, or even obstructions
for intelligence to overcome. (MW 9 1980, pp. 224–25)

Each of these areas captures a central truth about the social scientific
study of human conduct; that this is best done through examination of the
problems, concerns, needs, wants, and desires of peoples in their ongoing
struggle with their environment, and each other. Human problems, in short,
are the legitimate starting point for the study of the social sciences, and
social problems in the here and now are the best place to begin the long
look back into the past.

HOW DOES INQUIRY IN
SOCIAL SCIENCE EDUCATION OPERATE?

In general, social science education operates according to the same pattern as
inquiry in other contexts and that is to say, experimentally. I say in general,
because looked at closely, there are some telling differences. To say that social
science education generally follows the pattern of all inquiry is to say that
it begins with an unsettled existential situation, out of which a problem is
found and defined, then anticipated consequences of actions performed are
developed, followed by propositions and conceptions formed, leading to testing, and finally, the existential situation transformed. However, looking closely
reveals the problems, the consequences, the propositions and conceptions,
and the existential situations all differ from those in other contexts.

To begin with, the existential situation is understood to be a human
situation, not a physical one. A human problem is a problem that humans
have, with their materials, their environment, or one another. This differs
in role and scope from a physical problem, which is a problem that is often
seen in isolation from human conduct. Why would the fur trade take on
such significance in seventeenth-century Canada? How might the invention
of a steam engine help Americans become more geographically dispersed?
Why might some peoples have a problem with a foreign army occupying
their country—even if it is there to help? When existential situations are
seen to involve concerns bearing directly on human conduct and concerns,
these are from the hypothesis, social scientific situations. In spite of the fact
that most scientific research occurs at one remove from human affairs, once
this is placed in its larger context, the human aspect of even this becomes
apparent. It is in this sense that all scientific research is ultimately social
scientific research.

A human problem is not so much discovered as announced. Take the
example of hunger. If a segment of the population is hungry, calls will go out
to others to alleviate this plight. A problem in a social scientific context is

often self-identified: those with the problem will speak up. Of course, this does not always happen. Those that feel uncomfortable or pressured may not be allowed to speak up, and then problem finding and solving become more difficult. This does require access to resources and to methods to obtain and understand these. Beyond this, aggressive investigation of the existential situations of others is called for. This has led some to claim that social scientific research is engaging in politics. I shall deal with this concern in the next section.

Once a human problem is identified, anticipated consequences are developed. Universal, hypothetical conceptions are formed ("if we do this—then that should happen" conceptions) and potential strategies are weighed against each other in the context of the situation. Novel concepts and propositions are formed. These concepts are universal, but only in the sense that they operate to further the goals of inquiry. In some social sciences, ideal types of existent or anticipated situations are developed. Terms such as "community," "society," "democracy," "race," "class," "gender," "culture," "civilization," "invasion," "occupation," "charity," "wealth," "poverty," all began this way. They have had their worth demonstrated through helping to solve human problems.

Existential propositions guide specific interventions. These relate directly to the existential situation at hand. These propositions signify action on the part of the researcher. For example, an existential proposition for dealing with poor student performance on standardized tests has been to incorporate test-taking skills specifically suited to these tests. A particular action or approach is deemed appropriate, and is attempted. If it is successful according to the criteria for acceptability in that situation, then it continues to be used. If not, then it is discarded and a new existential proposition or set of propositions is developed. Evaluation of both conceptions and propositions are dependent on the solution to the problem at hand: the testing does not stop until the existential situation is settled. What counts as settled existential situations involving human problems is the alleviation of the concern or issue that first prompted the people to state that they have a problem. Admittedly, this is hard to follow through in a classroom setting, but microexperiments within the class and community can be developed to test out anticipated consequences. Science education has used the opportunity to grow plants and raise farm animals for generations; helping a child to understand a survey instrument or conduct an interview to gauge opinions can be done with as much facility.

This raises the question of how far the interventions developed in social scientific research are to reach. Technically speaking, a human problem is not solved until those that have the problem are satisfied. This is an existential, not a conceptual, matter. A problem may be satisfied conceptually (we know what to do) but not existentially (we have the wherewithal to do it or to follow it through to satisfaction). Until it is existentially solved, however, it is not truly solved. Widespread social problems, for example, poverty, hunger, addiction, homelessness, racism, and homophobia do not get solved through the development of human rights language, or commitments for more funding, or philanthropy and charity, or social programs to address these, until those that have the problem reach a settled existential state. Until then, new conceptions, new propositions, and ongoing evaluation are mandated by inquiry.

Of course, social scientific research in education does not have so grand a responsibility. It seeks rather to develop the habits of inquiry to the degree that students can see how a social problem can be solved, what the resources necessary for the solution to these are, and a beginning understanding of the various techniques and methods needed to carry this out. But it does seek something more. Beyond the acquisition of habits and skills of inquiry, there is the human element: the desire to see natural and physical problems in the context of social situations, and the desire to use nature to help people to solve these. We may call this desire, intelligently developed and applied a virtue. It involves other features or characteristics, such as empathy, the capacity to inquire, interpersonal skills, and a community in which these are developed and practiced. It is this virtue, necessary for democracy, that Dewey thinks students should cultivate through engaging in social scientific inquiry.

Dewey's examples in *Democracy and Education* are focused on bringing out the human elements implicit in the natural and physical sciences. There is no need, Dewey thinks, to invent arcane situations and contexts, when the use of technology and method is itself proof of the richness of social interaction. The very fact that peoples have and use materials to effect a change in their existential situations is already sufficient proof that these contexts provide wonderful opportunities to investigate human relations. To develop the social bearings of tool-use is to set the development of technologies in the context of the societies and civilizations that used them, and to ask the questions, why were they developed, how were they developed, what were these people trying to do with them, how did they or did they not, benefit from them, and how did other societies and civilizations take these developments up, use them, and change them for their own needs. These concerns are fluid with the scientific understandings of the technology at hand.

CONFLICTS AND DOUBTS IN SOCIAL SCIENCE EDUCATION

There are three conflicts and doubts I deal with here. The first is the doubt that social scientific inquiry can be successful and at the same time be value-laden. The obverse of this doubt (I shall consider these together) is that social scientific inquiry is entirely too scientistic, in that it borrows wholesale the methods and techniques of the physical and natural sciences.[9] The second and third problems are educational: the second is the doubt that social scientific education can really do what it intends according to Dewey—to help students grasp the problems of past and present peoples with the materials common to the schools in such a way that they will have the desire to do so.[10] The third is perhaps the most troubling: given social scientific research (and education) is not value-free, is in and is to be in, the service of human problems, does this not imply that social science research and education are political? If so, why should we support this?[11]

Perhaps the most common doubt regarding social science education arises in regards to how scientific it should be. On the one hand, Dewey tells us that the border between fact and value is fluid, or permeable, and that no scientific result, strictly speaking, is value-free. This seems to suggest that the normative aspects of all scientific inquiry receive their due. On the other hand, Dewey tells us that social-scientific inquiries lack something the physical sciences have long had: rigorous methods. And these methods are necessary for social sciences to become respectable, which for Dewey means helpful. This latter call has led many commentators to charge Dewey with scientism: the wholesale adoption of physical and natural scientific methods into the social sciences. There is some truth to this: in at least one respect, Dewey wants social scientific methods to emulate natural and physical scientific methods—in terms of their rigour and their operational ability. But this is not the same as saying Dewey wants the same methods to be used in social scientific situations. In fact, he calls for new and different methods, while at the same time maintaining these should be rigorous. The futility of quantifying observation reports or interviews should be evident: there is simply no good way to reduce a complex existential situation into a tidy numerical unity, quantifier, or pattern, and think that something meaningful has been said about that situation.

This still leaves social scientific inquiry with a paradox: how can a value-laden social science be depended upon to produce accurate, generalizable facts? How, in other words, can we trust the results of social scientific inquiry if these are tainted by the ends they are put to; to wit, the solutions to social problems. The paradox as it stands contains what we may call a smuggled premise: that scientific inquiry of the natural and physical varieties is somehow value-free. But Dewey shows us that this is not the case. All inquiry, regardless of its level of abstraction, is value-laden in the sense that it arises out of a certain context, and is developed for a certain end or purpose. It only seems to be value-free and this only happens when we detach the results of inquiry from the existential situation from which they develop. But once we do that, we render the chances of science being helpful in solving social problems, dubious.

The second concern is that schools do not have the intellectual or material wherewithal to carry out social scientific research. Much social scientific inquiry, it is said, requires access to people: if we are to study human relations, we must study people firsthand, and this seems impossible from the point of view of the classroom. Likewise, helping students draw appropriate intellectual conclusions from the material at hand seems difficult, given the lack of available, original source materials, and the lack of adequate research, library, and archival material at a school's disposal. Even if the point of social scientific inquiry is to help solve social problems, the requirement that these material considerations be in place seems to inhibit the possibility of carrying out such a program.

Again, there is some truth to this concern. There is no better standard for the purposes of conducting social scientific inquiry than to have original source material, or human subjects. This is, sadly, unlikely to happen in public schools. The best that most schools can offer is some original source material (as is found in anthologies or compendia, or in some cases, internet searches) together with firsthand narrative accounts of human interaction and the contexts in which the children are themselves in—the classroom. Nevertheless, the concern as it stands misses Dewey's point: that what is important is not to hunt for established social scientific materials, but to develop out of existing situations those existential aspects of social-scientific worth. Put differently, it is to see and develop the connections between persons and world in such a way that these can be augmented to benefit humanity. This can be done through examining the past uses of technology, for example, or role playing the problems earlier peoples have had, in the classroom, and this does not require access to considered social-scientific material. This material is ready to hand.

The final concern is that in relinquishing the value-free status of social science, we are surreptitiously introducing politics into the curriculum and classroom. Because the task is to develop out of existential situations an understanding of how peoples have coped, and bring this understanding to bear on current problems, the question of value judgments immediately arises. And if this is the case, we are putting students in the position of making value judgments regarding what amounts to social problems. This, it is said, is a political undertaking. To make value judgments with regards to social problems is tantamount to making claims on the public (often implying the taxpayer) and state (often implying various social institutions) for redress or amelioration, even though relational, to say nothing of causal, evidence that such a problem exists is not universally accepted. Social problems, for example, intergenerational poverty, the lack of health care, and environmental degradation, are not agreed upon problems—in terms of either their degree or the acceptable means to define them, let alone their solutions (if indeed there are solutions to these) and it is presumptuous, or so it may be claimed, to make social-scientific pronouncements on these. If this is the case, we are involving our students in politics.

To this, Dewey must plead guilty. For it is precisely to ameliorate social problems that social scientific inquiry is undertaken. Of course, Dewey does not (nor should he) make apologies for this: for Dewey, ameliorating social problems follows from the fact that we are social beings. Dewey's goal is to have enough communication, enough shared problem-solving, and enough shared experiences that social problems are amenable to solutions. The divide between social problems and politics is, for Dewey, a specious one. We just value certain practices over others, and the practices Dewey thinks we should best value are those in the service of solutions to social problems. This is cold comfort for many; particularly those that think public institutions have no business whatsoever exposing children, not to say teaching them, to see the need for social amelioration. Again, Dewey is not apologetic.

CONCLUSION

Social science inquiry shares the same general pattern as do all forms of inquiry. The investigation into an unsettled existential situation; problem-finding and defining; the development of anticipated consequences of action; the production of conceptions and propositions; and the testing of these in existential contexts, are all present. Nevertheless, there are some telling differences between social science inquiry in education and other forms of inquiry. Social science inquiry in education deals with human conduct and the problems it investigates are the problems of men. Physical and natural problems are not foreign to social science research, but what is specifically investigated of them is their bearing on peoples' behaviours and conduct, relations in groups, institutions and organizations, communities, societies, nations, and civilizations. Social science research is value-laden: it attempts to improve the existential situations of peoples and thus has as its end, a state of affairs that is existentially and experientially better than the one prior to investigation.

CHAPTER FOUR

Inquiry in Art and Art Education

Thus far we have spoken of inquiry in general, as well as in the specific contexts of (natural and physical) science and social science. Chapters 4 and 5 look at inquiry in seemingly odd contexts: art and movement (kin-aesthetics): Chapter 4 deals with art and chapter 5 deals with kinaesthetics. What distinguishes art from other contexts is the attention to doing and making (poēsis). There is a divide between knowing (epistēme), and doing and making. This divide is of ancient Greek origin: we find its beginnings in the works of Plato and Aristotle. For example, in Aristotle, theory (contem-plation) is said to be higher than doing and making. Theory is considered closest to the enduring and necessary laws and purposes of the universe, while doing and making depend upon the former. Doing and making, in contrast to theory, do not rely as heavily on logical or metaphysical truths, and for this reason, they are not as privileged. Dewey likes to make the connection between theory and doing/making on the one hand, and the wealthy, leisure classes (the contemplative classes) over against the artisans (the working classes), on the other. Dewey believes that class stratification is behind much of the vaunted superiority of theory, as only those that can occupy positions of leisure in society are able to obtain this knowledge (MW 12, p. 88; LW 1, p. 76–77).

Yet even the ancient Greeks must admit that doing and making are necessary pursuits for the construction of a society, particularly for its trade, infrastructure, architecture, et ceterea. Further, they must admit that the trades are necessary for objets d'art, and the literature and music that we produce, consume, and judge as beautiful. Beyond this, they must admit the pervasiveness of doing and making; these are responsible for much of the culture and are everywhere present. Consider the Parthenon in ancient Athens: though it is an edifice constructed by thousands of artisans and labourers, it stands as a testament to Greek civilization and culture. This is just the claim that Dewey wants to make in his two texts dealing specifically with experience—*Experience and Nature* and *Art as Experience*. There is no metaphysical separation between the arts of doing and making and the arts of knowledge. They have different functions, and are distinguishable from one another, certainly: but their beginnings and endings are to be found in an existential situation, *not* in a logical determination.

WHAT DOES INQUIRY IN ART CONSIST OF?

Before I discuss the specific role of inquiry in art, I want to discuss what inquiry looks like in an experience. Dewey says that an experience is something had, undergone. Experiences roughly correspond to the existential situations that we discussed in chapters 2 and 3: we are in a situation, and in that situation, we have an experience. The experience is satisfying or it is not. If it is not satisfying, we attempt to change the experience to one that is satisfying, much the same way we change an unsettled situation into a settled one—with the help of inquiry. Indeed, inquiry functions in both capacities and contexts to effect similar results because inquiry is the means we use to change both situations and experiences. Inquiry is the common thread running through each of these. In discussing the role of inquiry in experience then, we alter our language to say that inquiry is the means or tool we have and use, to bring satisfactory experiences about.

When we have an experience, we note qualities. These qualities are immediate; they are not abstracted or deduced.

> Immediate qualities in their immediacy are . . . unique, non-recurrent. But in spite of their existential uniqueness, they are capable, in the continuum of inquiry, of becoming distinguishing characteristics which mark off (circumscribe) and identify a kind of objects or events. (LW 12 1986, p. 248–49)

Qualities help us to identify events. We obviously prefer events having satisfying qualities. The business of inquiry is to pick out these qualities, and order and control these such that they occur in other existential situations. Likewise, disagreeable traits are mitigated or factored out. Here is the best single—paragraph explanation from Dewey's *Logic* I can find regarding the role of experience in inquiry.

> Discrimination occurs because of consequences of agreement and difference—because agreements and exclusions are instituted by recurring operations in the experiential continuum. The outcome is that the presence of certain immediate qualities is so conjoined

with certain other non-immediate qualities that the latter may
be inferred. When this further operation of inference takes place,
the potential generality, due to the presence of the same modes
of change and activity is actualized. The resulting inference is
grounded in the degree to which differential consequences are
instituted so that some conjoined traits are inferable while other
traits are excluded. (LW 12 1986, p. 250)

Inquiring in the context of an experience involves discriminating between
satisfactory immediate qualities and others. Satisfactory immediate qualities run
together with nonimmediate qualities and we infer (associate) these with the
satisfactory qualities in further experiences. When we infer, we have in place
a tool that we can use to manipulate the experimental situation for further,
satisfactory experiences. If a satisfactory immediate quality consists of the twitch
of a frog's leg, and one of the conditions that this takes place under (say, the
general position of the electrode on the leg of the frog), is conjoined with
this, we can infer that the latter has direct bearing on the former.

In *Experience and Nature*, Dewey calls these immediate qualities, "the
generic traits of existence." These traits are, ". . . qualitative individuality
and constant relations, contingency and need, movement and arrest . . ."
(LW 1 1981, p. 308). These traits are expanded by Dewey in *Art as Experience* to include, ". . . our constant sense of things as belonging or not
belonging, of relevancy, a sense which is immediate" (LW 10 1987, p. 198).
These qualities

cannot be a product of reflection, even though [it] requires
reflection to find out whether some particular consideration is
pertinent to what we are doing or thinking. For unless this sense
were immediate, we should have no guide to our reflection. The
sense of an extensive use and underlying whole is the context
of every experience." (LW 10 1987, p. 198)

We have, then, qualitative immediacy and constant relations, contingency
and need, movement and arrest, and belongingness, as the generic traits of
existence. These are not constructed or made by inquiry or reflection; these
are natural, and arise in every existential situation and it is these, Dewey
tells us, which we manipulate to occasion further, better experiences.

Now, one might think that certain sorts of experiences are, in terms
of their qualities, better. This is correct. Aesthetic experiences, in particular,
are considered the highest sorts of experience. The question is, what makes
an experience aesthetic, and why is an aesthetic experience the highest sort?
The answers to these questions might surprise us. For one thing, an aesthetic

experience is what Dewey calls consummatory: (LW 1 1981, p. 273). It is a complete experience, one in which all of the traits of existence are at their maximum. But (and here is the surprising part) one cannot have a complete, consummatory experience without having done a great deal of practical and intellectual work. Not only is armchair science inimical to consummatory experience, but mindless making and doing is, as well. For a consummatory experience to occur, one must have making and doing, and reflecting and intelligence, operating at their maximum. Indeed, Dewey thinks of these latter as arts in their own right. Not only is there an art of doing or making; there is an art of thinking, reflecting, and investigating. This is because these are tasks that we do; they are activities, not objects. We certainly use different skills and techniques in doing these; but this does not change the fact that inquiry itself is an art. As Dewey says, "It is hardly worth while to oppose science and art sharply to one another, when the deficiencies and troubles of life are so evidently due to separation between art and blind routine and blind impulse" (LW 1 1981, p. 270).

This is not to say, though, that art and science are coeval: indeed, Dewey at one point in *Experience and Nature* claims:

> But if modern tendencies are justified in putting art and creation first, then the implications of this position should be avowed and carried through. It would then be seen that science is an art, that art is practice, and that the only distinction worth drawing is not between practice and theory, but between those modes of practice that are not intelligent, not inherently and immediately enjoyable, and those which are full of enjoyed meanings. (LW 1 1981, p. 268–69)

Theory and practice come together over what is satisfactory, what is meaningful, what is intelligent. Indeed, Dewey proclaims that if these implications are followed through science "is properly a handmaiden that conducts natural events to this happy issue" (LW 1 1981, p. 269). Note that the functional role of science is to aid art in the development of better experiences. Science, properly considered, is the means to do this, and this allows us to draw some conclusions about the relationships between the two of these. First, science without art is empty; by itself, it has nothing to work on, and as such, cannot lead us to better experiences. Second, art without science is blind; without science to set legitimate ends in and for existential situations and discriminate amongst the better and worse experiences we have in these, making and doing has no direction.

We are now in a position to see what is different about inquiry in the context of art and aesthetic experiences. I note three differences here, and take these up respectively.

1. The focus on the constructive and experiential aspects of inquiry; more so than in other contexts and particularly, the presence and use of imagination and emotion in inquiry.

2. The task of inquiry in the context of doing and making: the manipulation of materials.

3. The different techniques and methods in the context of art: specifically, the use of experimentation to produce an art object.

I begin with the first difference. As I have said, art is doing and making. When we do art, we construct something. The contexts in which art takes place are wide ones, and they include not only the traditional (painting, literature, sculpture, music, and drawing) but the ordinary (building, cutting, welding, erecting, repairing, and manipulating) and the intellectual (thinking, imagining, reflecting, relating, and communicating). One might think of all the tasks that a small child does in the space of a morning in the classroom: drawing, painting, manipulating toys and other objects, running, playing, and interacting and communicating with her fellow students and teacher, cutting and pasting. The point is that all of these are arts and to engage in them is to be artistic. We might say that the context of art is inclusive of other contexts, if this was not so broad a description of art as to be uninteresting. But art is unique in this: that its goal (at least for Dewey) is the deepening and enriching of an experience. To make art or to experience art already made—both of these lend themselves to enriched experiences if the qualities had of that experience are at their maximum. Making, doing, acting, and thinking are integrally fused in this and this fusion is characteristic of all art, intelligently carried out. The focus shifts from a set of techniques or skills (though these are certainly important as means to ends) to the ends of experiences themselves. Likewise, the point and purpose of art as a bona fide subject-matter is to help students develop the skills necessary for the enrichment of their experiences.

Central to all of this is the role of imagination and emotion. We have previously noted the centrality of these, and that imagination and emotion cannot be separated from the task of inquiry. What does it mean, though, to privilege imagination and emotion in an inquiry? Does this mean we should choose sentiment over inquiry? Emotion, Dewey tells us,

> belongs of a certainty to the self. But it belongs to the self that is concerned in the movement of events toward an issue that is desired or disliked. We jump instantaneously when we are scared, as we blush on the instant when we are ashamed. But fright and shamed modesty are not in this case emotional states. Of themselves they are but automatic reflexes. In order to become

emotional they must become parts of an inclusive and enduring situation that involves concern for objects and other issues. (LW 10 1987, p. 48–49)

Emotion arises in an inclusive (existential) situation in which desire of something (or someone) takes place. This is why art excels at evoking emotional responses: artists "build up a concrete situation and permit it to evoke emotional response. Instead of a description of an emotion in intellectual and symbolic terms, the artist "does the deed that breeds" the emotion" (LW 10 1987, p. 73). We often see this in children that successfully complete their tasks, not to say create something new. We might even say that emotion in this case is a terminal event; it is the organisms' completion of the satisfying experience.

Emotion, then, is a complex of reflex and desire or repulsion. We often use the term, feeling, to denote the state we are in. But we must use this term with a caveat: feelings are never unaccompanied states: they always exist in the context of a desire or repulsion. They are part of an existential situation. The trick is to use emotions intelligently. What does this mean? Dewey says,

> One may cry out with joy or weep upon seeing a friend from whom one has been long separated. The outcome is not an expressive object—save to the onlooker. But if the emotion leads one to gather material that is affiliated to the mood which is aroused, a poem may result. In the direct outburst, an objective situation is the stimulus, the cause, of the emotion. In the poem, the objective material becomes the content and matter of the emotion, not just its evocative occasion. (LW 10 1987, p. 74–75)

Artists harness emotions: they harness their own emotions first-hand, when producing a work of art. And they help us to harness our emotions by invigorating them so that we may then get control of them. Artists help us to train our own emotions by their example. When we arouse our emotions through an expressive object or through doing and making, it is because we are producing satisfactory experiences; we are having a complete experience. Our generic traits of existence are at their maximum. It is not that emotions confer the status of completeness on our experience; it is rather that the quality of our experience brings forth our emotions. If we understand which emotions are aroused by certain practices and contexts, we can improve and/or manipulate these to our satisfaction by producing objects that become the instigators of these. This is how emotions can be harnessed for the good of an experience. If this is right, art provides benefits for the control and channelling of vital forces.

Imagination plays a central role in producing art. As Dewey says:

It is not so generally recognized that a similar transformation takes place on the side of 'inner' materials, images, observations, memories, and emotions. They are also progressively re-formed; they, too, must be administered. This modification is the building up of a truly expressive act. The impulsion that seethes as a commotion demanding utterance must undergo as much and as careful management in order to receive eloquent manifestation as marble or pigment, as colors and sounds. Nor are there in fact two operations, one performed upon the outer material and the other upon the inner and mental stuff. (LW 10 1987, p. 81)

An artist deliberates with inner images even as she produces outer ones. There is a great deal of behind the scenes inquiry going on here; inquiry that takes place while the artwork is being produced. This takes the form of imaginative rehearsal, whereby anticipated consequences of acting in a certain manner on the medium are thought out before they are attempted in vivo. In this case:

Whether a musician, painter, or architect works out his original emotional idea in terms of auditory or visual imagery or in the actual medium as he works is of relatively minor importance. For the imagery is of the objective medium undergoing development. The physical media may be ordered in imagination or in concrete material. In any case, the physical process develops imagination, while imagination is conceived in terms of concrete material. Only by progressive organization of 'inner' and 'outer' material in organic connection with each other can anything be produced that is not a learned document or an illustration of something familiar. (LW 10 1987, pp. 81–82)

Dialectic is in play here: imagination develops the actual performance and the actual performance leads to further, imaginative inquiry: each is reciprocally ends and means to the other. This is artistic experimentation, and this is what inquiry, properly undertaken, looks like in the context of art.

Artists have various media at their disposal: paints, brushes, canvas and wood for painting, silk for silk screening, clay, copper, glass, and paper, et cetera, for each of these associated arts, as well as less orthodox media such as computers for animation or graphic design. When we include literature (word processors, paper), music (scores, instruments), and theatre (costumes, sets, an audience, dancing, singing, and venues), we begin to see the almost inexhaustible media in and upon which artists work. When we take into consideration the materials contemporary artists use (buildings, bridges, dams, forests), we see the almost inexhaustible media artists work with. The artist has almost the whole of nature as her canvas. From the trades—peoples that work "high in air on girders, throwing and catching red hot bolts" (LW 10 1987, p. 5), to the sculptor in her studio, art is taking place.

This, however, is not the understanding of artistic media in many schools. Often, schools focus on traditional media and traditional artistic expressions in their curricula when they do discuss art. Contrary to Dewey's notion that life itself is art, most schools excel at inculcating in children an appreciation of certain art: a very conservative because narrow appreciation if they do this. This is not to say that children should not be introduced to fine arts, as I will henceforth call these, but that art classes can be expanded to include many, many more media than they otherwise do. Thankfully, artistic inquiry does occur; often in settings that are manifestly not self-consciously artistic, such as in literature classes (writing or attempting to understand a play), technical or shop classes (designing and building a simple machine), and in physical education (playing a sport).

Artistic inquiry occurs whenever a conscious attempt at experimenting with media for the purposes of enacting a favourable, satisfying, and settled situation, is undertaken. As art is making and doing, the sorts of situations artists are involved in are constructive ones: something is being erected, produced, developed, or finished. Often this is a tangible, material, object—an expressive object, as Dewey calls it. Nevertheless, a literary product, even a philosophical product, also counts as an artistic product for Dewey; doing and making are not distinct from thinking and reflecting. Literature, poetry, creative writing, the essay, and songs are all legitimate products of art. The products of inquiry as products are as legitimate as the glass and paper revealed as an objet d'art. The traditional bifurcation of intelligence and art is behind the insistence that these are distinct activities.

As with a scientist, an artist has a repertoire of techniques and skills at her disposal. Often, these are psychomotor skills: certain controlled ways and means of using one's fingers, hands, and legs, to effect a desired change in the medium. These are built up as habits, and in their development, require conscious attention. Beyond this, artists are skilled in the knowledge of the properties of their media, their tools, paints, chisels, kilns, torches, software programs, et cetera. These implements are put to use in solving the artistic matter at hand. If the problem is to create a prespecified expressive object, then anticipated consequences are entertained, and various solutions are tried out. Those that work, those that lead to an aesthetically pleasing or satisfying actions, remain, while those that do not, are jettisoned. As with a scientific experiment, artists also problem-solve and in so doing use the techniques and methods common to their modes of inquiry.

Beyond this, the sorts of conceptions and propositions artists develop and use differ from those experimenting in the sciences and social sciences. The expressive nature of the artwork is obviously most important to the artist, and the qualities of the experience are foregrounded. Abstract conceptions, while useful to art historians and aesthetic theorists, do not play as great a role in the contexts of artistic inquiry as they do in, for example, physical science. This is not to say that there is little or no role for these; but often the role is contextual. That is to say, it is supplemental to the practicing artist. Knowing something of chiaroscuro is very valuable when one is trying to emulate a certain painter (for example, Caravaggio), but perhaps not as valuable when one is trying to gain psychomotor mastery over a certain technique. Often, the more abstract conceptions are dealt with after the student has at least rudimentary skills and knowledge in place. Nonabstract conceptions and propositions in art are often in the service of a certain response; evocative (or even provocative) images are anticipatorily produced before being inscribed onto the media. Often this anticipation is a pictorial representation, rather than a series of premises and conclusions.

WHAT CONTEXTS DOES INQUIRY
IN ART EDUCATION OPERATE IN?

In *Democracy and Education*, Dewey discusses art education in relation to educational values. We should take note of this: what counts as artistic is not the medium that is worked on (though this is certainly important) but the kind of experience obtained. Dewey puts it this way:

> It is . . . a serious mistake to regard appreciation as if it were confined to such things as literature and pictures and music. Its scope is as comprehensive as the work of education itself. The formation of habits is a purely mechanical thing unless habits are also *tastes*—habitual modes of preference and esteem, an effective sense of excellence. (MW 9 1980, p. 244)

Indeed, Dewey is concerned that a too rigid classification of experiences will lead to limitations of contexts conducive to the development of taste. This is a central concern of Dewey's in any educational context.

> The engagement of the imagination is the only thing that makes any activity more than mechanical. Unfortunately, it is too customary to identify the imaginative with the imaginary, rather

than with a warm and intimate taking in of the full scope of a situation. This leads to an exaggerated estimate of fairy tales, myths, fanciful symbols, verse, and something labelled 'Fine Art,' as agencies for developing imagination and appreciation; and by neglecting imaginative vision in other matters, leads to methods which reduce much instruction to an unimaginative acquiring of specialized skill and amassing of load of information. (MW 9 1980, pp. 245–46)

Dewey is asking for less restrictive contexts so that appreciation, estimation, and satisfaction may occur more regularly and frequently than they do. It is these contexts, and not the specialized contexts in which fine art is discussed, viewed, and practiced, that Dewey considers authentically artistic. This is not to disparage traditional contexts in which fine art is practiced; it is rather to open it up to other contexts so that they, too, may help develop the appreciations and estimations that artistic contexts already do for those so inclined. Doing this would mean having every classroom consciously guided so that some artistic context is introduced, and at least some traits common to artistic contexts, developed.

This may be a difficult pill to swallow, for it suggests that specialized art classrooms are less preferable than classrooms wherein art is integrated into the curriculum. Art and music teachers rightly prize their classrooms and the sorts of experiences these engender, and no doubt, do not want to lose these to integration, particularly as integration looks less expensive than maintaining specialized classrooms. Nevertheless, this is what Dewey suggests, and he has very strong arguments for this; the strongest of these being the narrowness occasioned by rigid constraints on what counts as art, and the effect that this has on the capacity of a child to benefit from varied media. Dewey would much rather see a classroom in which art is discussed in relation to history, geography, and mathematics, indeed, human problems. Art is very often a solution to these problems, an emotional release, and a means of making meanings that exemplifies what is best about a culture, a civilization, and deserves, therefore, to be front and centre in discussions of these other contexts. Nevertheless, this is not to say that there is little role for art teachers: ideally, both art classes and integration take place.

Let us take the example of a history class in which students learn to understand the various factors influencing trading between the European settlers and the native population in Eastern Canada. Part of the lesson might be devoted to producing native artworks that were offered as trade gifts. Doing and making is in evidence here: doing and making that enrich the experience of learning. The curriculum in this case is naturally extended to cover artistic topics and practices, and these are well within the context of the history lessons. Another example, this one from the physical sciences, might be the design of a hot air balloon in miniature to replicate the invention of the Montgolfier brothers. Designing and constructing the balloon, working out the fuel mixture, testing the balloon, calculating the forces involved in various environments—all of this makes the chemistry or physics lessons more meaningful. Mathematics has its artistic charms: calculating the amount of lumber, nails, screws, as well as the cost, and the load bearing capacities of materials to build a clubhouse as well as drafting the blueprints and the geometry this requires. The context here is artistic; doing and making are front and centre; but the means are mathematical and physical-scientific; arithmetic, geometry, and elementary mechanics are in play.

HOW DOES INQUIRY IN ART EDUCATION OPERATE?

The above gives us some idea of how inquiry in the context of art education is to operate: it is to be part of an integrated curriculum, serving an integrated lesson, in which many other subject matters are in play. What remains is to discuss how artistic inquiry is conducted. I remind us that what separates an artistic experience from other experiences is, first of all, the primacy of making and doing, and secondly (and perhaps most importantly) the quality of experience obtained. In fine, it is a complete and consummatory experience that is sought after. Artistic inquiry in education will have these features about it.

To begin with, artistic inquiry has the same experimental goals as other inquiries: to arrive at a settled situation. We note an unsettled situation; perhaps we have a goal or drive that compels us to construct or improve something from some material or medium. For artistic inquiry to be genuine it is vitally important that this unsettled situation be a genuine one; the child must own the situation, as well as the desire to change it. All is lost if this crucial step is omitted. The best way to ensure that a genuine situation obtains is to fasten on a topic or task within the context of the lesson that interests and engages the student(s). Problem-finding and problem-solving are central ingredients as well. The problem found must also be genuine, and the solution must be the child's own. Anticipated consequences are then thought out and tested, generally on the medium itself; evaluation of the results often ends in attempts to improve upon the consequences, not to say the product. A finished product is one that settles the situation, and (most importantly) obtains the desired satisfaction of the student(s). The student, not the teacher, is ultimately the one that pronounces the experiment a success.

Note what is required here: Time and lots of it, for the student to adequately consider her medium, its qualities and characteristics, opportunities to define the situation, choose the medium and the project one wishes to carry forth, and experimentation upon the medium itself; opportunities for reflection, and for imaginative rehearsal of various ideas;. A great deal of flexibility and discretion on the part of the teacher is required to ensure this. Classrooms must be set up in such a way that constraints on media and materials are minimized. Unlike other subject matter, art is profoundly student-centered (though not always individually student-centered) and this means that the students carry the lion's share of intellectual and imaginative responsibility for the projects undertaken.

Beyond this, certain techniques intrinsic to the medium and to the intended effect upon it, must be developed. These do require a fine arts teacher. As with the techniques of measurement, accuracy, precision, and astute observation of the physical sciences, artistic contexts demand certain techniques. Often these are psychomotor in nature, habituated through practice until automatic. Exquisite familiarity, for example, with different brushstrokes is a goal of long-term instruction in painting. Students begin to learn these techniques as they encounter and work with their media. Other techniques include foresight; the ability to see an image or picture of what it is one desires beforehand. This is both unique to, and central in, artistic inquiry. Finally, a certain sort of temperament must be developed; a patient temperament that is strong in terms of imagination yet is not so easily satisfied. Doing one's best ultimately promotes the satisfaction had, and the ability to remain unsatisfied with one's work—to continually strive to better oneself—leads to more profound experiences.

CONFLICTS AND DOUBTS IN ART EDUCATION

Despite the opportunities art education offers, creating an environment in which a maximum of satisfaction is attempted is no easy feat. Many, many ingredients have to be in place, and this is particularly difficult given the low budgets, limited resources, and negligible media at the disposal of teachers and classrooms. Indeed, these alone constitute compelling reasons for some to doubt the capacity of art education to make good on its offer. There are other, less obvious doubts, though, that I want to focus on here. One of these concerns the end or purpose of art education: if this is to be found in the satisfaction of an experience had, why can we not simply allow children to maximize their satisfying experiences by more direct, and less costly, routes? Why invest in art education when other media and other contexts can do this just as well?[12] Another concern is the nature of the other ends we are in pursuit of. We want children to not only have satisfying experiences, but learn something as well. Learning, as we all realize, is often a hard-fought battle, and significant progress does not often come easily. How can it be that a satisfactory experience had leads to learning, when much of what children need to learn is foreign, indeed, odious to them?[13] I shall deal with these in turn.

To begin with, it seems as if Dewey is saying that what counts in learning is the quality of the experience had, and this is true. However, to leave it at this, to not suggest how a quality experience is had, is to leave out a crucial aspect necessary to forestall the above objection: for satisfactory experiences lead to satisfactory meanings, and satisfactory meanings are what we want a child to take away from her experiences. Let me explain. When a child inquires, she does so for the express purpose of deepening and enriching her experience through the build-up of generic traits of existence. In so doing, the child develops meaningful patterns of responding, meaningful concepts and propositions, and meaningful techniques and methods of inquiry. It is these patterns, concepts, propositions, techniques, and methods of inquiry that education is after. These are in the service of heightened experiences; but it is important to note that experiences, for the purposes of education, are also in the service of these meanings. In *Democracy and Education*, Dewey famously calls the aim of education, "growth" (MW 9 1980, p. 46–47). Growth is the development of habits of inquiry such that ordering and control of the traits of existence can occur for the purposes of deepening and enriching experiences had. We are to visualize this process as a circle; a circle in which meanings, patterns, concepts, propositions, techniques, and methods of inquiry lead to further, better experiences, and these further and better experiences lead to further and better meanings.

The above forestalls the objection that art education is merely in the service of promoting satisfactory experiences. Learning occurs when the settled products of inquiry are consciously constructed and used in further situations. After time and practice, these become habitual; we no longer need to think about our responses to certain situations. It is when new situations, and specifically, new problems arise, that we become conscious once again of our need to investigate; to inquire. It is at this point that growth begins. Art education offers us the best hope of an environment and media that is conducive to growth: by bringing the entire organism to bear on the situation at hand, through making, doing, thinking, and reflecting, we augment the satisfaction of an experience had. We increase the chances that the experience will be complete, or consummatory. We offer the best opportunity we have to encourage the development of meanings, and the sorts of inquiry that are necessary for said meanings to develop. The best education is one that is holistic: that brings the entire child, body and mind, together in attempting to solve a problem or settle an unsettled situation.

This leads to the further concern, why fine arts and music programs are so frequently dismantled. Clearly, in the minds of those that make fiscal decisions, the arts assume a secondary status in comparison with literacy, numeracy, and other so called salient subjects. Sadly, one unintended consequence of a Deweyan approach to fine arts education might be to suggest that since the regular classroom (and teacher) has everything it needs to help children develop aesthetic experiences and appreciation, fine art teachers are unnecessary. However, as I previously argued, this is false: fine art teachers and programs are as necessary as math and science teachers and programs. Often, teachers have little knowledge of the fine arts, little understanding of art history, and even less understanding and skill in working with media. Art teachers have all of these, and can lead children in directions teachers without these skills and knowledge cannot. Art teachers can act as a resource for others that do not have the skills and knowledge at their disposal. Not only do art teachers offer children with interests in pursuing art and art history, art teachers help to provide the cultural glue that holds civilization together, in the form of expressions, symbols, and meanings.

CONCLUSION

Let's put it all together. Inquiry in art and art education offers the best opportunity to develop complete and consummatory experiences. This is because inquiry in art is holistic: it emphasizes making and doing as well as thinking and reflecting. Both body and mind are engaged in art, and the direct manipulation of media enhances this. Satisfactory experiences had are the touchstones of genuine growth: to develop better and richer experiences is the goal of inquiry in this context. Inquiry operates to facilitate this process: meanings are developed that lead to better and richer experiences, which lead in turn to better and more fully develop meanings. In this way, a loose circle of meanings and experiences is formed. Inquiry in art education does not require specific or particular media to carry out: it only asks that situations and problems be genuine, and that the child has a great deal of opportunity to work out the details of anticipated solutions.

CHAPTER FIVE

Inquiry, Embodiment, and Kinesthetics in Education

One of the central features of inquiry that has not been discussed is its embodied nature. Inquiry is not simply an affair of the mind; it is an affair of body as well. Indeed, it is an affair of the total organism. We should not be surprised at this, given Dewey's insistence that an organism responds in an existential situation, and not an abstract mind or intellect: an organism undergoes change as a result. Dewey's naturalism, his biology and psychology of adjustment, is in full force here: we adapt to our environment through changing our environment to solve social problems. Dewey sometimes discusses the oneness of the organism and environment as a reflex-circuit. We constitute, together with our environment, a circle in we reciprocally affect one another.

> Take the withdrawing of the hand from the candle flame as example. What we have is a certain visual-heat-pain-muscular quale, transformed into another visual-touch-muscular quale—the flame now being visible only at a distance, or not at all, the touch sensation being altered, etc . . . The motion is not a certain kind of existence; it is a sort of sensory experience interpreted, just as is the candle flame, or burn from candle flame. All are on a par. (Dewey 1972, p. 103)

Notice that the immediate experience we have is not confined to the quale of pain; it is organic, and consists of the quale of seeing (vision), touching and feeling (pain), and motion (moving). In this reflex circuit, we do not just think—we react in, and to, the existential situation in which we find ourselves. Thinking and reacting run together the way making, doing, inquiring, and reflecting, run together. The point being that a complete act

71

involves all of these. When we experience, we experience the whole circle of seeing, touching, feeling, and moving. Thinking, inquiring, and reflecting are the logical outcomes of a reflex circuit that are then integrated into that circle for the benefit of future events. They become, in short, part of the reflex circuit. What I attempt to do here is discuss the role of the body in undertaking an inquiry and the role of inquiry in education of the body/mind.

Dewey talks about the importance of the body in several odd, yet revealing, contexts. One of these is in relation to the technique of F. H. Alexander—the so-called, Alexander technique. Dewey had been struggling for many months with chronic back and neck pain, and on the advice of Alexander (who had written to Dewey), began treatment. The treatment consisted of a series of exercises, and deliberate control of posture. Dewey's comfort apparently improved considerably, and henceforth, he praised Alexander and his technique, and even wrote a forward for Alexander's first book. Alexander's thesis was that the crisis of conflict between the functions of the brain and other body systems recapitulates itself in the crises of morals, economics, and politics, and is responsible for the somatic complaints of a large number of the population. The solution to these was to reeducate the body/mind to work in concert, rather than conflict. Dewey puts Alexander's thesis this way.

> Mr. Alexander contends that our education, which covers, of course, infinitely more than our schooling, has proceeded as if the centres of conscious activity had been merely superimposed upon the neuro-muscular structures which represent our heredity from the lower animals. As a result we get evils which are unknown to the animals and to the savages whose intellectual achievements have not become sufficiently complex to override the animal functions. But civilized persons, especially the intellectuals and specialized persons who are leaders, cultivate their 'brains' as if they were separate from the rest of the body. . . . The net outcome, in Mr. Alexander's contention, is the larger number of physical disorders which inflict themselves exclusively upon civilized man, and the large number of neuroses which express themselves in intellectual and moral maladies. (Dewey 1972, [pp. 353–54)[14]

Dewey's forward to Alexander's book, *Man's Supreme Inheritance*, is revealing: Here is what Dewey has to say with respect to the body's influence on the mind and the mind's on the body:

> In his criticism of return or relapse to the simpler conditions from which civilized man has departed Mr. Alexander's philosophy

appears in its essential features. All such attempts represent an attempt at solution through abdication of intelligence. . . . The pitfalls into which references to the unconscious and subconscious usually fall have no existence in Mr. Alexander's treatment. He gives these terms a definite and real meaning. They express reliance upon the primitive mind of sense, of unreflection, as against reliance upon reflective mind. Mr. Alexander sees the remedy not in a futile abdication of intelligence in order that lower forces [subconscious or unconscious] may work, but in carrying the power of intelligence further, in making its function one of positive and constructive control. (Dewey 1982, p. 351)

If Dewey (and Alexander) is correct, this (re)education of the body/ mind may well be central to the establishment of genuine inquiry into social problems. This education, if it were to take hold early, might alleviate the stresses Alexander and Dewey discuss. At least, Dewey certainly believed so.

WHAT DOES INQUIRY IN BODILY-KINESTHETIC EDUCATION CONSIST OF

The word "kinaesthetic" derives from the Greek terms, kinesis and aesthesia, and combined, these roughly mean, movement-sense. Bodily-kinesthetic education is most obviously distinguished from other sorts of education in its attention to touching, feeling, and movement. However, this is not all: as important as these are, equally fundamental is an awareness or perception of one's body in space. This is called proprioception, and it is a legitimate sensation. Proprioception is the outcome of the combination of brain, nerve endings, particularly in the limbs, certain spinal nerve tracts, and the vestibular apparatus in the inner ear that controls balance. Competent proprioception demands exquisite attunement to one's surroundings and this in turn requires practice at a specific skill or set of skills, involving what is in effect, a reflex circuit of body and mind.

Consider the mechanics of a gymnast on a balance beam: literally hundreds of minute adjustments take place in the span of a few seconds for a single turn to be executed, and this requires conscious, deliberate attention to one's position in space at each stage of each movement. Until this complex of sensation, attentiveness, and movement becomes automatic, the reflex circuit is not complete, and the movement is not fully perfected. One might think that little thought, little reflection or intelligence, is required for such an activity; this is profoundly mistaken. A great deal of thinking takes place; dozens of adjustments have to be anticipated, attempted, reworked, reattempted, and ultimately, settled upon. Much conscious deliberation is required of the athlete in these circumstances. The point is that this is as much a cognitive affair as it is a bodily one and those athletes that do not actively experiment do not succeed at their task.

It comes as no surprise, then, that there are techniques and methods, as well as practices and contexts, unique to inquiry in bodily-kinesthetic education. These are:

1. The focus on sensations and movement, either with or without, implements, involving the deliberate control of body parts.

2. The context, which often involves (though not always) physical exertion and possibly, spectators or an audience.

3. The sorts of techniques and methods that one uses to improve ones' performance and the performance of others.

4. The differing criteria of experimentation in bodily-kinesthetic inquiry.

I shall take these up in sequence. Dewey does not talk a great deal about bodily-kinesthetic education per se; he does talk a great deal about the need to coordinate psychomotor skills with thought and reflection. Famously, he talks of the need for young children especially, to remain active. In fact, Dewey discusses this is several different contexts; education, art, experience, scientific inquiry, and child development. We have seen this, for example, in our discussion of art. Indeed, one of Dewey's greatest and ongoing criticisms of education at the time was the separation of the body from mind into lower and higher spheres, respectively. Dewey never stopped insisting that carving out the intelligent functions human organisms execute and setting these off in a realm where they are trained in isolation from the body, constituted on of the most egregious practices in schooling.

Nevertheless, because Dewey does not specifically address bodily-kinesthetic education, we must make some assumptions as to what it might look like. Here, the focus is on tight synchrony between mind and body. Thought, sensation, and movement are inextricably linked together. Much practice is involved in getting the psychomotor skills down to the point where they become almost effortless; indeed, automatic. As the focus is on the movement of the body, extra attention is placed on the sensory and motor apparatus; specific feels and positions are noted and calculated. The presence of one's limbs in space is acutely felt and noted. Stresses and strains on muscles and joints are common in these and other activities, and exquisite attention to prevention of injury is a necessary corequisite to the attentiveness on body position.

Implements add yet another dimension to bodily-kinesthetic education, and often represent another set of skills to develop. Consider the situation of a hockey player. The hockey player must not only learn how to skate, but also must practice consummate eye-hand coordination, stick handling, obtaining the puck from opponents, blocking access to the goalie, as well as taking appropriate penalties, body checks and falls without injury, this in addition to shooting the puck. The seamless connection between the player, stick, ice, and equipment, must be fluid for these skills to develop to a maximum. Likewise, a tennis player must be attuned to the court surface (many good hard-court players do poorly on clay), the racket, the particularities of an opponent's serve, the wind, and the density of the fabric on the balls. And this is in addition to the tennis player's position in space. Any implement added to the repertoire of an athlete requires much additional time and practice to integrate fully.

The contexts in which bodily-kinesthetic education takes place are myriad. Here, I note the often-times public nature of this education. Frequently, students are watched while they develop their skills, and certainly when they are competing. For many, this is another skill to master. Beyond this, there is the stress of performing in certain venues, such as plays or dances, where an audience is often present to watch the performance. The fear of being in public must be overcome and the tendency to show off or to freeze must be managed. Unfortunately, bodily-kinesthetic performances can be frightening because tight control of other students' remarks and manners is often not enforced. More than one child has refused to participate in gymnastics or team sports because of a fear of being singled out or made fun of.

Techniques and methods common to bodily-kinesthetic education include warm-up exercises, such as stretches, cardiovascular or aerobic fitness, such as jogging, swimming, or running; and practice plays, drills, and scenarios, as in team sports. There are more techniques and methods than activities, and I can only discuss these in general terms. These often involve attention to factors beyond those associated with classroom education. The most important technique for the purposes of bodily-kinesthetic education is to practice bodily self-awareness: the position of oneself and one's extremities in space; the proper handling and use of implements; and the proper attention to one's inner sense. Beyond this, proper eating and diet, proper rest, scrupulous attention to overuse, injuries or illness, checkups with one's physician, appropriate warm-up exercises, techniques for muscle strengthening, prevention and management of falls, and proper hydration, are common for the vast majority of these activities.

There are psychological techniques that are used as well in bodily-kinesthetic education. Some of the most common are positive reinforcement, encouragement, team-building, and rewards and prizes. I refer to the

competitive nature of much bodily-kinesthetic education more fully in the
final section of this chapter. For now, though, there are techniques favoured
by many coaches, parents, students, and athletes to encourage motivation
and esprit de corps. Competition for prizes and rewards is basic to many
team and individual sports. It is also basic to much physical education in
schools. Indeed, students often compete among themselves irrespective of
whether teachers assign formal rankings to them. Competition often plays
the role of the unsettled situation in bodily-kinesthetic education: Who
will be first or win?

The kinds of experimentation that go on in bodily-kinesthetic education vary greatly with the activity undertaken. I note only the role experimentation in general has to play in this. To experiment in these contexts
ultimately means to try out new techniques, new methods, new angles or
ways of approach, all in the service of improving one's performance. The
methods and techniques are generally psycho-sensory-motor, and they involve
the unity of body (sensation and position; movement) and mind. The success of a chosen technique is measured in the overall performance: if the
performance is enhanced, the technique is likely to be integrated; if not, it
is likely to be discarded in favour of another. Problems in bodily-kinesthetic
education are usually related to a specific deficit (often noted by an astute
teacher or coach), and at least in athletic and many team-sport contexts,
are religiously scrutinized, and, as is the case in college-level, Olympic, or
professional contexts, specialists in exercise physiology, athletic therapy, or
kinesiology are called on to improve the player's performance. These specialists use the body of research and knowledge common to these sciences,
in this capacity. Often they are available to high school students, both in
team and individual sports.

WHAT CONTEXTS DOES INQUIRY IN
BODILY-KINESTHETIC EDUCATION OPERATE IN?

I look at three contexts in some detail, here. The first is team sports. The
second is dance. And the third is theatre. Though these contexts vary
widely, we shall see that they have much in common in terms of the bodily-
kinesthetic knowledge necessary to their performance. Players on sports teams
typically spend a great deal of time learning how to work with one another
in split-second situations. This requires frequent and intensive practice. In
addition to the various skills required for each of the positions played, the
skill of teamwork, broadly considered, is of paramount importance. Teams
usually work together in other ways as well. They often socialize with one

another in a variety of contexts such as meals, rallies, fundraising, and parties. This is to help build esprit de corps. In this way, the context of bodily-kinesthetic education is integrated with the context of team—that is, as a social context. Much anticipatory work is put in to obtain a stellar performance: the execution of successful plays requires much deliberate, thought-out planning and often this is done in conjunction with the other members of the team. Often, in team sports, a coach is involved in this stage of deliberation, but this does not obviate the player's responsibility for her own role in deliberating her performance. Within the context of larger strategies exist smaller, individual ones; these each player has, or is to have, control over.

The second context I examine is dance. There are surprising similarities between dance and team sports: often, members play a part in a larger sequence of events that must take place, and each dancer has her own role to perform within this sequence. As well, there is a premium placed on bodily-kinesthetic awareness. There is also direction, often from a choreographer, or dance coach, to develop strategies of execution in tandem with the dancers. There are habits and techniques unique to dance. However, one of the main differences is the rhythm a dancer must maintain. This is often done in conjunction with, or to, music. Planned synchronous or asynchronous (depending upon the nature of the dance) movement is the goal. Regardless, attention to pace, timing, cadence, and tempo, are mandatory. Dancing involves a great deal of repetitive stresses and strains on certain muscles, bones, and joints—specifically, the feet and ankles, which necessitates meticulous warm-up exercises, and close attention to injury prevention. There is also the public nature of much dance: often, dance is performed in and for, an audience. Though this is often the case with team sports, dancers tend to be front and center so to speak, as they are generally performing on a stage, dealing with multiple skills (bodily-kinesthetic), but also musical, and social—requiring a seamless response from the dancer. These account for the complex challenges the dancer faces.

The final context is that of the theatre. Here, not only does the performer have the need to integrate bodily-kinesthetic, public, and musical skills into a fluid presentation, she has the additional skills of vocalization, characterization, and perhaps even singing to master. A great deal of practice performance, generally under the direction of acting, singing, and dancing and movement coaches, is required, and this is in addition to the basic choreography. Somehow, the performer must develop habits that integrate psychomotor, vocal, attention and memory, and social skills. These habits must become second nature. This requires consummate attention to each and all of the contexts the performer works in.

All of the above suggests that, far from requiring little in the way of intelligent, thought-out direction; performers such as these need this in abundance. No single skill takes place without thoughtful consideration of its consequences for other skills, for the venue, for the performance itself. A symphony of intelligent thinking, habit, sensing, and movement, is the hoped-for result of this consideration. Indeed, I believe that one reason why performances seem to lack the need for intelligent direction to outsiders is the seamlessness of the performance itself: One does not see the difficult, anticipatory work that goes into the performance; one sees only the result. It takes a great deal of anticipatory, indeed, focused, deliberation to make it look easy.

HOW DOES INQUIRY IN
BODILY-KINESTHETIC EDUCATION OPERATE?

Nowhere is the context so important to the ways in which inquiry operates than in bodily-kinesthetic education. Nevertheless, some general words can be said about what works with respect to building bio-psycho-motor skills. To begin with, there is a requirement that students come to a conscious awareness of their position in space. This involves developing one's capacity for proprioception; that is, awareness tied not only to the limbs, but also to the vestibular organs in the inner ear and the spinal tracts that flow to and from these. To become aware of this, indeed, to master this, requires one to subject oneself to a variety of different positions over time, and to practice these until one becomes conscious of one's position in space, and (most importantly) secure with this. The need to become self-conscious yet secure about one's position in space requires focused deliberation. One must learn to attune oneself to one's limbs in various spaces. As implements (hockey sticks, uniforms, baseball gloves, rings, balance beams, period costumes, and swords, et cetera), are introduced, these also need to be integrated into one's existing sense of balance and position, and this requires further deliberation and practice. Skill mastery in this context generally begins with the basics, meaning mastery of the most essential skills first. This includes balance, basic movements, rhythm and speed, et cetera. These are followed by increasingly difficult skills, or skills involving implements. Getting psychomotor skills down pat is to habitualize them; making them automatic and routine. Then new skills can be developed.

Experimentation is present throughout. When a figure skater tries out new moves, she experiments. When a football player adopts a new implement or attempts a new strategy with an old one, he is experimenting. When a dancer learns a new routine, or a theatrical performer tries a new vocal technique to sing a part, she is experimenting. When a baseball player tries out a new glove, he is experimenting. When a gymnast chooses to pause for a microsecond before executing a dismount, she is experimenting. What counts as a successful experimentation is the success of the move or technique; but this masks the behind-the-scenes deliberation and testing that is occurring. Much conscious attention (again) is put into this. There is a great deal of conception formation here: much of the anticipatory work is in the form of if I do this, or move this way, or sing at this octave, then I will achieve my desired response. These imperatives or general propositions (as Dewey calls them) are the means by which improvement in skill occurs. Such decisions do not first form mentally or linguistically, are then made conscious, and only after this, are attempted on the body. Rather, such decisions occur simultaneously; body and mind work together as one, taking the point of departure from habits already developed, in the development of new ones. It is best to think of inquiry in bodily-kinesthetic education as taking place in a circle. For example, a movement fails to produce its desired effect, leading to a problematic or unsettled situation; problem finding and solving begin (what is the problem and how shall I solve it?). Conscious deliberation (perhaps I will wait a half-second or two), anticipatory consequences (I believe if I do, I will dismount more smoothly), and finally, new or different movements, in the service of solving the problem or unsettled situation, are then undertaken (a microsecond's pause before the dismount). Existing (unsatisfactory) movement begets conscious deliberation, begetting transformed and satisfactory, movement.

To see the process of bodily-kinesthetic education in terms of a circle is educationally speaking, more sound than to see it in terms of a linear march from thought to action. Indeed, thought and action, or movement, are reciprocally ends and means for one another on this better view, and as such, demand that the whole situation, not just the mental or physical side of the situation, be examined and adjusted. In inquiring into problems for athletes, dancers, and theatre performers, it is most helpful to concentrate on the entire execution, including the context in which the execution takes place in, rather than on one isolated segment. Certainly, isolating segments is required, but this is to be done after an analysis of the execution as a whole, in its context, and not beforehand. As habits, thoughts, and movements are part of a seamless whole in a bodily-kinesthetic execution, each individual segment is bound up with another, and this fact cannot be overlooked. Any change in one segment, or a change in the context in which the segment of a movement takes place in, will likely result in changes for the others, and due attention to modifying all of these must be in place for success to occur.

CONFLICTS AND DOUBTS IN
BODILY-KINESTHETIC EDUCATION

Here, I discuss two doubts regarding bodily-kinesthetic education. The first is perhaps the most pressing. Given that bodily-kinesthetic education often involves contexts in which competition operates, and competition is not always looked on favourably (and often for good reason), how can we minimize the competitive nature of this education, while maximizing the benefits?[15] The second doubt concerns the value of bodily-kinesthetic education. For it seems that society at large does not value this heavily, or, if it does, it is valued for less than beneficial purposes (e.g., alumni relations, entertainment, fundraising) and certainly, it is less valued than traditional, academic subject matters.[16] If this is the case, why should schools invest in this education, particularly when academic pursuits are lauded more highly, and the costs of financing this education are high?

Competition is a problem that requires attention. Far too many children are placed in contexts that they do not wish to be in, or feel pressured to be in. The scenario of an angry coach or parent berating her or another's child is unfortunately, all too common. This sort of competition is at variance with the aims and purposes of public schools, and cannot be encouraged. Yet at some level, healthy competition seems important, indeed, necessary to motivate students, particularly those in team sports. I believe the key is to help the child develop the skill of self-motivation. This requires a thoroughly knowledgeable and attentive teacher or coach—perhaps a rarity in many instances. The techniques and methods of motivating children in this manner are beyond the scope of this book. None of this, though, necessitates the avoidance of bodily-kinesthetic education: while it may be that some activities are inappropriate for students, owing to a lack of resources or qualified staff (e.g., some team sports; gymnastics, a dance studio), this should not prevent teachers from finding ways to engage students in embodied activities.

A more difficult variation on this concern is the social ranking that occurs all too frequently in team or group-based activities. This is indeed a problem for any group activity, but where physical prowess is as esteemed as it is in sports, it raises particular concerns. Unfortunately, there is a fine line between the benefits of group exercise and group physical activities (which are well documented), and the losses incurred by stratification. Clearly, overt stratification (including, but not limited to, hazing, teasing, put-downs, name-calling) cannot be tolerated. The case, however, is less certain with respect to students choosing the members of their teams, or not inviting certain students to engage at the level of others. No child wishes to be singled out in this manner, yet this can be difficult to avoid. I am not of the opinion that this is something to be eliminated root and branch: I think that each particular case must be examined individually. But this means that adequately trained teachers and staff are present in large enough numbers for this, and this is in itself seems a difficult goal to reach.

The other concern is the value, or more properly, the lack of value placed on bodily-kinesthetic education. It seems largely to be off the radar for many school districts and indeed, state and provincial officials. True enough, there is rhetoric to the contrary regarding the need for more physical activity for children. Nevertheless, this rhetoric fades quickly in light of the real and perceived obstacles. Academic concerns generally take precedence, and this is nowhere more in evidence that with the fetish for standardized testing (one can only imagine the outcry if standardized testing of physical education took place, yet we are quite willing to allow it for literacy and mathematics). Physical education programs are among the first (as with art and music) to be cut and though almost no one would declare publicly that these are superfluous, the fact that they are so easily discarded speaks the truth to this. Many of these programs do cost money; team sports for example, cost a great deal of money, if we are to contrast these with, say, mathematics education. But there are two good retorts to this: the first is that bodily-kinesthetic education does not require extensive sports programs to be effective. The second is that there are multiple opportunities within the existing curriculum for bodily-kinesthetic education to occur.

Though many of the examples I have used suggest that bodily-kinesthetic education works best only in highly charged, tightly constrained, competitive environments, this is in fact not the case. While the experience gained in these contexts is debatably more complete than in less structured activities, the experience gained, the experience of the latter is more fulfilling, and more complete than one in which no bodily-kinesthetic activity is undertaken. Any opportunity to develop psychomotor skills with direction is a good one: for these skills are oftentimes transferable to other contexts—certainly this is the case with the attitudes developed. However, the enjoyment and satisfaction gained applying oneself in a holistic sense—body and mind—is itself a worthwhile end. Though we often forget this in our desires to be competitive and to win, it is the satisfaction of the experience had that is the proper goal of this education. Once that satisfaction disappears, or is stolen away, the very point and purpose of this education is lost. For the vast majority of students, this, and not superior performance, is the proper end of bodily-kinesthetic education. In the same way, we do not suggest all students become full-time or consummate artists, we do not suggest that all students develop superior athletic or performance skills. This is not our decision to make.

CONCLUSION

Bodily-kinesthetic education is an education in which body and mind are fused together in a seamless whole for the purposes of successful execution in the context of a complex activity such as dancing, team sports, or theatre. This execution takes the form of a reflex-circuit: sensations beginning in the body necessitate corresponding deliberation and conscious attention, leading to a change in bodily position; movement. The fluidity of this should not lead one to think that there is no attention being paid to one's position, or that anticipatory consequences are developed and in force: in fact, the obverse of this is the case. Heightened attention to one's position and numerous possible movements are executed both imaginatively and physically, in working out the desired effect. Experimentation is an ongoing affair in bodily-kinesthetic education. The development and refinement of the habits and skills of psychomotor control requires exquisite investigative work to undertake.

Conclusion

The foregoing chapters have discussed Dewey's theory of inquiry from the perspectives of varying contexts. In each of the areas discussed—science and science education, social science and social science education, art and art education and bodily-kinesthetic education—inquiry plays a central role. What counts as inquiry in each of these areas is dependent on the problems that arise, as well as the contexts that inquiry develops out of, and is beholden to. Regardless of the differing problems and contexts, inquiry operates to order, control, classify, and ultimately, enhance meanings and relations so that problems can be solved, enriched experiences can be had, and growth, both individual and social, can proceed.

Here, I bring forward the sum of my conclusions concerning how we may best understand Dewey's contributions to facilitate inquiry in educational practice. I do so in such a way that links all of the above areas together. These conclusions are in no particular order, but all are vital, on this reading, to the success of inquiry in the classroom.

1. We must ensure that an unsettled situation, a problem had is a genuine one for the student. This is the absolutely crucial condition. This generally requires the student to see the teacher's problem as her own, and/or develop her own sense of the problem. Ensuring that this happens is perhaps the most difficult and frustrating aspect of teaching. Nevertheless, it is necessary for further inquiry. It will happen only if a student is already familiar with the context, and possibly the subject matter, that the problem arises from, or is already familiar with a (developmentally appropriate) self-selected, personal variant of this.

2. Subsequent anticipatory consequences are the student's to develop and use, not the teacher's. Teaching concepts is misleading if what we really mean by teaching is imparting, or disseminating, or training. The analogy of the teacher passing along knowledge to the student fails in the case of concept learning. Concepts are those formalized operations that operate for the student, and

must be developed by the student. Abstractions and conceptions are notoriously difficult for children, and this is not because they cannot develop them. Rather, it is because they are given fixed and ready-made, with little or no context to the problem they were originally developed to solve, and little or no instruction as to how they were arrived at. Allowing the student the freedom to try out differing consequences in the context of a student-discovered, legitimate problem, is the best and easiest way to overcome this obstacle. Concept-formation, rather than concept-accumulation, is the goal.

3. Inquiry terminates in a settled situation—a satisfactory conclusion to the problem at hand, not in a predetermined, correct response, or the development of the right concept, statistical measure, or numerical unit. Inquiry does not end until the student is satisfied that the problem begun with is solved. Though a student may have produced the correct response, unless the student experiences the closure (cognitive and affective) that comes with settling the problematic situation, intelligent, educational growth has not occurred.

4. Inquiry practiced in public schools does not need to be, indeed often should not be, pursued in isolation. Seatwork is beneficial in those contexts where seatwork is a genuine feature of the problems under investigation. Group inquiry should be the norm in those contexts where inquiry in the real world occurs cooperatively.

5. Materials are valuable means to help a student develop her powers of inquiry, but the most complex or most expensive materials are often not needed. Indeed, less is often more here, as costs, the frequency of breakdowns, the difficulty to operate, etc., often militate against complicated and expensive implements. In terms of inquiry, the means are mistaken for the ends when the educational aim becomes one of facilitating tool use for its own sake, rather than for intelligent growth.

6. The best subject matter and contexts are often those the child is in already. It is easier and more conducive to student interest and effort to examine the scientific, mathematical, social scientific, aesthetic, or bodily-kinesthetic aspects of a topic already under discussion or investigation than to import a foreign one, or develop one anew. Furthermore, the integral nature of subject matters will be better established on this approach than if topics are dealt with in isolation.

With more attention to the attitudes, tempers, environments, and specific techniques and methods used, education can make valuable use of the knowledge we have already built up regarding inquiry. The issue is not one of ignorance, or of insufficient understanding of techniques to help children develop the skills that will make them productive, intelligent, and socially aware thinkers: It is rather the case of failure of the collective will. In order to establish such a program, all must be on board; this presumes that all see the value in, and are willing to undertake, changing educational programs to suit this end. Many do not. The reasons for this vary. Certainly, there are those that believe the proper role of the school is to impart knowledge, and train a child up. These do not constitute the greatest issue public education faces. A much more insidious, yet ultimately powerful force is at work. Ultimately, educating children, as with much else regarding children (day care, parental leave, family allowance, and preventative health care) is trivial and not deserving of rigorous investigation let alone compensation. Though we often say education is important to us (and certainly at the municipal and/or local government level), we allow experts and legislators to make decisions that weaken classrooms. Though we want our children to be educated, we are not willing to put in place the resources (the monies) required to ensure its success. The care of children is still tied tightly to conceptions of traditional female roles and work. This, I argue, has a great role in the relative unimportance of education. It surfaces in the waves of educational reform, specifically, the assignment of responsibility (but not authority) to the teachers and the students. What we are left with at the end of the day to overcome this state of affairs is the force of persuasion. Not unlike other needed changes in education, this too, requires stakeholders to be on board.' Whether this can happen democratically, and not by fiat, is a question that concerns all educators.

Notes

1. The history of education in America (excluding Canada) is one of dogged dedication to efficiency. From the 1920s onwards, schools have had as a leading agenda sorting children according to ability—innate and learned. Different explanations were given during different times. For example, during and shortly after World War I, reasons given included distinguishing officer material for the armed forces. Sorting mechanisms also identified the laboring classes: those that would populate the factories. In the 1950s sorting operated as well to distinguish those with scientific and technical acumen from the masses. Technological advances were necessary during the tensions of the Cold War, and education was seen as the means to provide these. In the 1980s and 1990s, international economic competition drove programs such as "A Nation at Risk," and "American 2000." Sorting, testing, and measuring students against each other was necessary to evaluate America's standing against other nations. The fear was, if other nations' educational programs were better than America's, these would profit economically, while America would decline. Placed in context, North American schools are doing quite well at producing human capital; the United States has most of the top one hundred universities in the world; it produces the greatest number of PhDs; many of the schools have state-of-the-art equipment, not to say, exemplary student performance. Indeed, there is a glut of overeducated, degreed individuals, many of whom cannot find employment commensurate with their education. The argument I am making is counter to the rhetoric of failure so common nowadays. Schools do a great job of educating children for North American needs; perhaps too great. For many children, however, they do a lousy job of fostering *genuine intellectual growth* of the sort Dewey recommends. We must not confuse the two.

2. I am using method and inquiry interchangeably. Dewey sometimes uses the term method in a general manner, to connote the established techniques, attitudes, tempers, and practices of those experimenting in varying contexts. He also uses inquiry, broadly speaking, in the same way.

3. Much educational literature regarding the need to develop interpersonal relationships has accumulated over the last two decades. The arguments here are partly Deweyan: learning takes place in the context of relationships, and is a significant factor in how well a child will understand material. Beyond this, relationships serve a valuable problem-solving skill: as much inquiry occurs in groups, developing the skills and attitudes to work competently and fairly in groups seems important. Nel Noddings, Jane Roland Martin, and others have identified the need for developing relationship skills and attitudes, particularly for boys.

4. There is no shortage of critics eager to pin anti-intellectual and scientistic charges against Dewey. Some of the most famous educators include Israel Scheffler, E. D. Hirsch, Diane Ravitch, and Kieran Egan. The basic argument is that Dewey does not allow for imagination or creativity in his problem-solving approach to inquiry. As a result, inquiry becomes largely a matter of experimentation. Again, the fallacy here is to understand Dewey's talk of experimentation as having nothing to do with emotion, imagination, or creativity. The best defense against these readings is found in Dewey's *How We Think*, 2ⁿᵈ edition, and *Art as Experience*.

5. Charges of anti-intellectualism, of dumbing down the curriculum, of replacing knowledge with activity, and the resultant failure of education to meet the needs of an increasingly global economic market, are legion. These attacks have been around for close to a century, and fresh variants (Hirsch, Ravitch, and Henry Edmundson III) are always to be found. The argument is never airtight: generally, it relies on an assumption of causality; that because education began to decline with the Progressivist movement, that therefore Dewey was responsible for this decline. Beyond this, what counts as 'decline' is not so much addressed as begged. Often decline devolves into one or another variant of whatever is opposite the educational view desired. As I said earlier, North American schools do quite a good job of educating children for human capital. What they do not do a good job at is fostering genuine, intellectual growth.

6. Bertrand Russell famously charged Dewey with paying insufficient attention to real facts and sense data. That there were facts and objects existing external to the mind Russell maintained against Dewey, whom he saw as arguing for a world captured only in an experience. At the height of logical positivism, Russell's accounting of Dewey was taken seriously; however, with the demise of logical positivism and empiricism, Russell's criticism is given little credence. The linguistic turn, the movement in philosophy beginning in the 1950s, that consigned all talk of real objects and data presented to the mind as mistaken, cast a cold eye on correspondence theories of knowledge.

7. Dewey has been implicated in a debate regarding the constructivist theory of knowledge. Constructivism, broadly understood as that theory claiming human beings construct knowledge through developing the logical powers of thinking (with Piaget) denies the arguments of realism; that there is a world out there, waiting to be had. The world is rather a construction that develops as the child grows. No doubt, Dewey's talk of growth and adjustment seems to place Dewey in this constructivist school of thought. As well, inquiry seems to do some of the work that is required to develop the logical powers of thinking. However, those that lump Dewey in with the constructivists ignore his statements on how experience is had and undergone. It is not the case that logic or mind constructs the experiences we have. There is no question of mind making nature. We just do have these experiences. What is constructed is the ways and means we deal with these experiences. Dewey does not admit the totalizing power of mental states that constructivists do.

8. A long debate, beginning in the 1930s, occurred between certain neo-humanists (Alexander Meikeljohn, Robert Hutchins) and Dewey over the aims and purposes of education. For the neo-humanists, schools were responsible for teaching

the Western canon, raising the child to appreciate and understand the achievements of western civilization and the great books and works of art brought forth as evidence of this. These thinkers accused Dewey of foisting a utilitarian and scientistic education on children, with the outcome being generations cut off from the rich legacies of the past, and fodder for industrialization and manufacturing. Dewey's reply was harsh: schooling children in the past for the sake of the past merely reproduces those barriers of race and class that effectively divide people, whereas teaching inquiry provides students with tools to break these barriers down.

9. There are variants of this charge as well. For John Patrick Diggins, Dewey's scientism is infected with relativism and an appeal to the present over and against the past, and traditions are said to be swept aside in Dewey's all-destroying scientific method. For Kieran Egan and Chet Bowers, Dewey's scientific method is anthropocentric; it has little concern for the environment, or for non-scientistic ways of being. None of the thinkers believes that Dewey's inquiry is capable of self-adjusting or correcting; all of them think that to be scientific is to be scientistic, and to be experimentalist is to negate the value of the non-human.

10. Some commentators believe that Progressive education fails not because it cloaks an insidious scientism, or that it is present—focused, rather that it has little in the way of tools to dismantle prevailing institutional power. The arguments here are that Dewey's scientific method gives us very little in the way of means to deconstruct ideology, hegemony, and entrenched power. Aaron Schutz is a good example of these thinkers. Dewey's reply is that it is up to the public, working together on shared problems, to do this. For many commentators, though, this is not enough.

11. Those not inclined to progressive practices will not be swayed by Dewey's insistence that scientific inquiry is the *best* way to solve social problems. For these, scientific inquiry (at least, Dewey's version) is already committed to a certain social-democratic (some might even say socialist) viewpoint: that the point and purpose of inquiry is to solve social problems. Add to this Dewey's lack of a place for traditional religion, and this looks, to these anyway, as a secular and relativistic program inimical to traditional teachings. It should not surprise the reader to know that Dewey's *Democracy and Education* is the fifth most subversive and dangerous work in America—ahead of Karl Marx's *Das Kapital*! David Horowitz's website has the complete details of this. http://www.humanevents.com/article.php?id=7591

12. To the best of my knowledge, this has not come up in recent educational literature, though it is an economic conclusion that could (and indeed most likely has) be made against art education.

13. The argument is as follows: children do not often like what they have to learn. If we teach children based on their motivations and interests, we will find there is little that we can teach them because most of what they traditionally learn is uninteresting. Further, the point of education is to train children to develop the habits of learning what they don't like, and if we don't do this, we are abdicating our collective responsibility to subsequent generations. The best way to answer this is to claim that this view rests on a begged premise: either a child likes what she is learning and will learn or a child does not like what she is learning and will not.

The problem with this premise is that it is faulty. Children often regurgitate material if they are compelled to, but significant learning does not take place.

14. This passage is from an open letter, published in the *New Republic*, commenting on Randolph Bourne's review of Alexander's book. Bourne's review is quite scathing; he accuses Alexander of charlatanism. In coming to Alexander's defense, Dewey reiterates the central thesis of the book.

15. This is a difficult and complex problem, which I can only touch on here. I suggest that one way to manage this is to remind ourselves of the point and purpose of school sports and athletics, which is to develop a sound interrelationship of body and mind. Goals or aims that are synchronous with this are generally acceptable. Those that are not, however, should be carefully thought through beforehand.

16. Critics of sports programs in schools have good reasons to be upset. Far too frequently, sports (especially team sports) take on a role out of proportion to the academic functions the school is supposed to provide. The problem with this is two-fold. First, academic pursuits get sidelined or downplayed. Second, monies that might have gone to fund academic programs or school infrastructure end up supporting the team. This leads to a disproportionate amount of attention to team sports. I am not saying that team sports have little or no place in schools. However, the point of team sports in a school setting is different from professional settings, community settings, or entertainment. Team sports in school settings are to develop a well-rounded individual that appreciates and pays attention to, both body and mind in the context of developing social skills and attitudes. This suggests a balance between academic pursuits and sports is the best equation for which to strive.

References

Bourne, R. "Making over the Body by Randolph Bourne. Review of Man's Supreme Inheritance." In *John Dewey: The Middle Works, 1899–1924*. Vol. 11, 1918–1919, edited by Jo Ann Boydston, 359–60. Carbondale: Southern Illinois University Press, 1982.

Dewey, J. "The Reflex-Arc Concept in Psychology." In *John Dewey: The Early Works, 1882–1898*. Vol. 5: 1895–1898, 96–110, edited by Jo Ann Boydston. Carbondale: Southern Illinois University Press, 1972.

———. "The Need for a Recovery of Philosophy." In *John Dewey: The Middle Works, 1899–1924*. Vol. 10, 1916–1917, edited by Jo Ann Boydston, 3–48. Carbondale: Southern Illinois University Press, 1980.

———. "Introductory Word to Man's Supreme Inheritance by F. Matthias Alexander" In *John Dewey: The Middle Works, 1899–1924*. Vol. 11, 1918–1919, edited by Jo Ann Boydston, 350–52. Carbondale: Southern Illinois University Press, 1982.

———. "Reply to a Reviewer." In *John Dewey: The Middle Works, 1899–1924*. Vol. 11, 1918–1919, edited by Jo Ann Boydston, 353–55. Carbondale: Southern Illinois University Press, 1982.

———. Experience and Nature. In *John Dewey: The Later Works, 1925–1952*. Vol. 1, 1925, edited by Jo Ann Boydston. Carbondale: Southern Illinois University Press, 1981.

———. The Sources of a Science of Education. In *John Dewey: The Later Works, 1925–1952*. Vol. 5, 1929–1930, edited by Jo Ann Boydston, 1–40. Carbondale: Southern Illinois University Press, 1984.

———. How We Think. In *John Dewey: The Later Works, 1925–1952*. Vol. 8, 1933, edited by Jo Ann Boydston, 105–352. Carbondale: Southern Illinois University Press, 1986.

———. Art as Experience. In *John Dewey: The Later Works, 1925–1952*. Vol. 10, 1934, edited by Jo Ann Boydston. Carbondale: Southern Illinois University Press, 1987.

———. Logic: the Theory of Inquiry. In *John Dewey: The Later Works, 1925–1952*. Vol. 12, 1938, edited by Jo Ann Boydston. Carbondale: Southern Illinois University Press, 1986.

Suggested Readings

For those who want to pursue the study of Dewey's notion of inquiry further, I suggest the following resources.

Burke, Tom. *Dewey's New Logic: A Reply to Russell.* Chicago, IL: University of Chicago Press. 1994.

Dewey's Logical Theory: New Studies and Interpretations, edited by E. Thomas Burke, M. Hester, and R. Talise. Nashville, TN: Vanderbilt University Press, 2002.

Hickman, L. *Philosophical Tools for Technological Culture: Putting Pragmatism to Work.* Bloomington: Indiana University Press, 2001.

Johnston, J. *Inquiry in Education: John Dewey and the Quest for Democracy.* Albany: State University of New York Press, 2006.

Manicas, Peter. "Pragmatic Philosophy of Science and the Charge of Scientism." *Transactions of the Charles S. Peirce Society* 24 no. 2 (1988) 179–222.

Shook, John. *Dewey's Empirical Theory of Knowledge and Reality.* Nashville, TN: Vanderbilt University Press, 2000.

For those who want to see the various criticisms of Dewey, I recommend the following texts.

Diggins, John Patrick. *The Promise of Pragmatism: Modernism and the Crisis of Knowledge and Authority.* Chicago, IL: University of Chicago Press, 1994.

———. "Pragmatism and its Limits." *The Revival of Pragmatism: New Essays on Social Thought, Law, and Culture,* edited by Morris Dickstein, 206–31. Durham, NC: Duke University Press, 1998.

Edmundson III, H. *John Dewey and the Decline of American Education: How the Patron Saint of Schools Has Corrupted Teaching and Learning.* Wilmington, DE: ISI Books, 2006.

Mounce, H. O. *The Two Pragmatisms: From Peirce to Rorty.* London: Routledge, 1997.

Ravitch, D. *Left Back: A Century of Battles Over School Reform.* New York: Touchstone, 2000.

Russell, B. *The History of Western Philosophy.* London: Unwin. 1979.

Scheffler, Israel. *Reason and Teaching.* New York: Bobbs-Merrill, 1973.

———. *Four Pragmatists.* New York: Routledge and Kegan Paul, 1974.

Schutz, Aaron. "John Dewey's Conundrum: Can Democratic Schools Empower?" In *Teachers College Record.* 103 no. 2 (2001) 267–302.

For those who want to see Dewey's theory of inquiry at work in schools, I recommend the following resources.

Bloom, J. *Creating a Classroom Community of Young Scientists.* New York: Routledge, 2006.

Fishman, S. and McCarthy, L. *John Dewey and the Challenge of Classroom Practise.* New York: Teacher's College Press, 1998.

Garrison, J. *Dewey and Eros: Wisdom and Desire in the Art of Teaching.* New York: Teacher's College Press, 1997.

Jackson, P. *John Dewey and the Lessons of Art.* New Haven, CT: Yale University Press, 1998.

———. *John Dewey and Philosophic Method.* New York: Teacher's College Press, 2001.

McCarthy, C. "Deweyan Pragmatism and the Quest for True Belief." *Educational Theory* 50 no. 2 (2000): 213–28.

Meier, D. *The Power of their Ideas: Lessons for America from a Small School in Harlem.* Boston, Beacon Press, 1995.

Tanner, Laurel. *The Dewey School: Lessons for Today.* New York: Teacher's College Press, 1997.

Volk, S. *A Democratic Classroom.* Portsmouth, NH: Heinemann, 1998.

Waks, Leonard. "Experimentalism and the Flow of Experience," *Educational Theory*, 26 no. 2 (1998): 1–19.

Index